MIDI Editing in Cubase®:

Skill Pack

Steve Pacey

THOMSON

COURSE TECHNOLOGY

Professional ■ Technical ■ Reference

MIDI Editing in Cubase®:
Skill Pack

Publisher and General Manager, Thomson Course Technology PTR: Stacy L. Hiquet

Associate Director of Marketing: Sarah O'Donnell

Manager of Editorial Services: Heather Talbot

Marketing Manager: Mark Hughes

Acquisitions Editor: Orren Merton

Marketing Assistant: Adena Flitt

Project Editor: Kate Shoup Welsh

Technical Reviewer: Casey Kim

PTR Editorial Services Coordinator: Erin Johnson

Copy Editor: Kate Shoup Welsh

Interior Layout Tech: Judith Littlefield

Cover Designer: Mike Tanamachi

CD-ROM Producer: Brandon Penticuff

Indexer: Sharon Shock

Proofreader: Gene Redding

Cubase is a registered trademark of Steinberg Media Technologies GmbH. All other trademarks are the property of their respective owners.

Important: Thomson Course Technology PTR cannot provide software support. Please contact the appropriate software manufacturer's technical support line or Web site for assistance.

Thomson Course Technology PTR and the author have attempted throughout this book to distinguish proprietary trademarks from descriptive terms by following the capitalization style used by the manufacturer.

Information contained in this book has been obtained by Thomson Course Technology PTR from sources believed to be reliable. However, because of the possibility of human or mechanical error by our sources, Thomson Course Technology PTR, or others, the Publisher does not guarantee the accuracy, adequacy, or completeness of any information and is not responsible for any errors or omissions or the results obtained from use of such information. Readers should be particularly aware of the fact that the Internet is an ever-changing entity. Some facts may have changed since this book went to press.

Educational facilities, companies, and organizations interested in multiple copies or licensing of this book should contact the Publisher for quantity discount information. Training manuals, CD-ROMs, and portions of this book are also available individually or can be tailored for specific needs.

ISBN-10: 1-59863-302-3

ISBN-13: 978-1-59863-302-3

Library of Congress Catalog Card Number: 2006906798

Printed in the United States of America

07 08 09 10 11 TW 10 9 8 7 6 5 4 3 2 1

THOMSON

COURSE TECHNOLOGY

Professional ■ Technical ■ Reference

Thomson Course Technology PTR, a division of Thomson Learning Inc. 25 Thomson Place Boston, MA 02210

http://www.courseptr.com

*This book is dedicated to the late Dick Grove
and the wonderful former teachers from the Grove School of Music.
Their patience and expertise in helping me learn and understand
MIDI and music was one of the most valuable experiences of my life.*

Acknowledgments

Thanks to Thomson Course Technology for giving me the opportunity to write this book and to everyone at Thomson who has worked hard in making this book a reality. Special thanks to Orren Merton, who put his trust in me and offered 100% of his support from day one. Thanks to Kate Welsh for her sharp eye for details, wisdom, support, and understanding. Thanks to Casey Kim for taking the time to check and recheck my wording and instructions to ensure that everything I've written makes sense. Also, thanks to Judith Littlefield for laying out this title, Gene Redding for proofreading it, and Sharon Shock for indexing it. Special thanks to Matt Piper, who not only offered his moral support as a friend, but also offered the wisdom and expertise of a great author. Also, thank you Matt for your kind words and recommendations to the wonderful people at Thomson Course Technology. Thanks to the people at Steinberg for continuing to take Cubase to levels I never dreamed possible when I first started using the program. I'd also like to thank the sales guy, whose name has long been forgotten, at West L.A. Music, who steered me in the right direction and gave me the deal of a lifetime on my first starter Cubase system in 1990. Special thanks to all my friends and family for their continuous love and support. Last but not least, thank you, the reader, for having the desire to learn and explore MIDI. Your desire will continue to fuel the future of music for generations to come.

About the Author

Steve Pacey has been interested in music since childhood. His desire to learn more about music took him from piano lessons; to playing trombone in the grade-school band; to writing songs; to rapping and learning how to beat box; to playing keyboards and singing in a rock band; to attending a specialized music school; to owning and working in recording studios; to writing music for theater, TV, video, and film; to producing bands; to editing music technology books; and, finally, writing this book. His first computer was an Apple IIe. He later moved on to an Atari 1040Ste and now he uses a Dell desktop with Windows XP. He has been a devoted Cubase user since attending the Grove School of Music, where he studied songwriting and recording engineering in Los Angeles in 1990. He currently writes and produces music for several TV shows, including the television series *The Ultimate Blackjack Tour* on CBS. He's a member of ASCAP and NSAI, owns his own music-publishing company (Spot On Music) and recording studio, and lives in "Music City," Nashville, TN, where he continues to write music for fun and for a living.

Table of Contents

Contents

Introduction

MIDI: The Music Producer's #1 Music-Creation Tool

Back in the 1980s, when computers were just beginning to be used to make music, people thought computers added a different and exciting new element to music. These days, however, if you're not using a computer at some point during the music-creation process, it's as though you're going against the grain. The fact is, computers have come a long way since those early days. More and more, they've become a crucial part of the recording community. Indeed, these days, the "dream" recording studio consists almost entirely of computer equipment, as shown in Figure I.1.

Figure I.1

Today's dream studio.

This explosion in the use of computers among recording engineers can be credited in large part to the development of MIDI. Short for Musical Instrument Digital Interface, MIDI (pronounced "mid-dee") was invented in the early 1980s by synthesizer manufacturers to enable various synths and hardware sequencers to "talk" to each other, regardless of who manufactured the device. Put another way, MIDI was developed as a universal language for synths.

Undoubtedly, a lot of musicians frowned on MIDI when it came out. After all, this new technology put some musicians, such as string players, drummers, percussionists, composers, and even keyboard players, out of a job. Where were these jobs going? To the guys who *embraced* the MIDI technology. Some composers, music producers, keyboard players, and programmers just couldn't get enough of the new technology. In fact, it was MIDI that inspired two guys in Germany to form a small business in the early 1980s to design a software MIDI sequencer that, one day, would become one of the most powerful tools in music creation. Today, that company is know as Steinberg, and the software is Cubase.

Nowadays, MIDI isn't just for synth pop dance bands or nerdy-looking guys with ties. MIDI is now used in just about every style of music: pop, rock, heavy metal, rap, hip-hop, country, dance, classical, jazz, Latin, polka—even reggae! You name it: MIDI has been there, and will continue to be there for a good while longer. This explains why today, most music producers and composers need a professional understanding of MIDI technology.

Why MIDI? As mentioned, MIDI is a universal platform. Almost every cell phone, computer, and video-game system plays MIDI files. Moreover, in addition to being supported by all pro music software as well as by hardware such as synths, MIDI files are used on the Internet, with video applications, and more. In short, MIDI is everywhere.

Digital audio has since drawn alongside MIDI as a leading tool in music recording. The development of digital audio started with samplers, followed by digital tape recorders, CD players and burners, MP3s, and iPods, culminating with technology that enables just about anyone to make high-fidelity digital recordings using their home computer. Together, digital audio, MIDI, and a robust computer system (not to mention digital video) yield virtually limitless recording possibilities—at a price that's a fraction of what an eight-track analog tape recorder cost just 25 years ago.

Cubase 4: Virtually Limitless MIDI Possibilities

Every program has its limits. But Cubase, a tried-and-true program that has been imitated by every software developer in the industry (even Cakewalk, which came out before Cubase, was ultimately re-designed to be more like Cubase after Cubase's release in 1989), gives you more freedom to push those limits. Don't get me wrong: I like a lot of other programs on the market. Reason, ACID, and WaveLab are all great at doing certain things. But none of these programs can hold a candle to Cubase.

So what makes Cubase so attractive, especially in the way it handles MIDI? First, Cubase can do absolutely anything that is possible in a MIDI sequencer. Second, the program's platform, essentially unchanged since the program's creation, makes musical sense (see Figure 1.2). Plus, you can use Cubase to seamlessly integrate your MIDI with high-quality professional digital audio, to interface with other musicians through the Internet, and to export MIDI files. Using the program's virtual instruments and third-party software, you can pretty much carry around an entire studio, capable of creating any of the top-40 songs out there today, in a portable laptop computer. Cubase is really only limited by *your* musical and technical limitations.

What to Expect from This Book

I've worked as a music producer for TV and video for a decade, used Cubase for 16 years, explored MIDI for 20 years, and played music for 25 years. I even attended a specialized music school when I was 18. Even so, if I told you that I could teach you everything there is to know about MIDI in this book, I'd be lying, or nuts!

Figure I.2

MIDI and audio recording in Cubase 4.

What I can tell you is this: Other than having some basic music-theory knowledge a drive to learn, and a desire to experience everything possible in both the art and business of music, the best thing you can do is learn about computers, MIDI, and digital recording. Whether you're a harmonica player, a tuba player, a keyboardist, a guitarist, or a DJ, the more you know about computers, MIDI, and digital recording, the better off you'll be. In fact, these days, you need to consider the computer as an instrument in itself.

This book has been designed specifically for the musician who owns and is acquainted with Cubase 4. Even though the Cubase manual contains a lot of valuable and useful information, its structure and details on MIDI editing are lost in a virtual sea of technical information. Here, I have tried to simplify and organize the MIDI side of Cubase in a way that should make better sense to even the most MIDI-fearful musician. This book includes a CD-ROM with pre-recorded music, enabling you to walk with me through every MIDI edit in order to help you better understand the program.

The book starts slow, picking up momentum as it goes. Specifically, it shows you how to use Cubase to edit MIDI in every possible way. It also touches on how to create MIDI notes and events, use MIDI effects, create a MIDI score, quantize MIDI, and export your MIDI as a digital audio file. That said, there are a few things you *won't* find in this book. You won't find much coverage of digital audio, the play order track, the Tempo track, the mixer, the control room feature, surround sound, automation, audio processing, the MediaBay, ReWire, video, synchronization, scoring, or virtual instruments. I'm sorry, but I just can't squeeze all that into this little book. For information on these subjects, check out other Cubase titles published by Thomson Course Technology.

> **NOTE**
>
> Although I understand that some of you may want to jump around in the book, skipping ahead as you read, I'd like you to try to resist. Instead, read the book from beginning to end. You'll see that knowledge of the basics covered in the early chapters will be necessary as the book progresses. If you skip a section, you may find yourself lost later on.

System Requirements

I hope this book provides you with the building blocks necessary for using MIDI in the way that works best for you, and reveals aspects of Cubase that you would have never discovered on your own. To achieve that, here's what you're going to need:

■ A computer (Windows or Mac)

> **NOTE**
>
> This book was written using the Windows version of Cubase. If you are using a Mac, you will likely need to translate some of the Windows-specific wording to work for you. If you need help, you can find the necessary translations and other relevant information on page 14 of the Cubase manual.

■ At least 1GB of RAM

> **NOTE**
>
> The demo songs I've created use Cubase 4's virtual synths, which can take a significant bite out of your RAM; for this reason, the more RAM your computer has, the better off you'll be. You should be alright with at least 1GB of RAM in your system. I currently have 2GB, and I have no problems using Cubase.

■ A legitimate and working copy of Steinberg's Cubase 4 program, installed and running on your computer (it won't hurt to have the Cubase manual handy as well)

■ A CD-ROM drive

■ A mouse (preferably with a wheel)

■ A MIDI keyboard controller (preferably with at least 49 keys)

■ A pro sound card with MIDI and an audio monitoring setup (headphones will work if necessary)

NOTE

When I say "pro" sound card, I'm not talking about the card that came with your computer—although you may be able to get by with it in a pinch. There are several pro sound cards available by manufacturers such as M-Audio, Digidesign, Tascam, and so on. Personally, I find that Steinberg's sound cards work best with Cubase.

■ Optional (but highly recommended): Dual monitors

TIP

Because there are so many variations in computers, MIDI keyboards, sound card setups, you should refer to your manuals to ensure that everything is installed properly.

Of course, knowing everything there is to know about editing MIDI in Cubase is great, but the only way to become a Grand Master at MIDI editing is to practice and use the program on a regular basis. I'll point you in right direction, but the rest is up to you.

A Quick Look at the Key Editor

A company named Steinberg, formed in the early 1980s, developed the MIDI sequencer known as Cubase in 1989. Although Cubase was not Steinberg's first MIDI sequencing software on the market, it reinvented the way musicians and recording engineers looked at MIDI software. Indeed, since its release, Cubase has become a model for every other MIDI sequencing software on the market. And although a lot has been added to the program over the years, the basics of MIDI editing in Cubase are pretty much the same as they were when I began using the program in 1990, on an Atari 1040 STe computer.

Before Cubase, most software sequencers, like many of the hardware MIDI sequencers of the day, were *looped based.* That is, they worked by repeating a section of music over and over again, enabling you to add or remove elements of the arrangement as the section looped. Cubase enabled you to look at a song as one continuous piece of music from start to finish rather than in sections. The program also offered more options for editing MIDI. Most importantly, Cubase made MIDI much easier for the less technically experienced musician to understand.

Although Cubase offers several different editors for working with MIDI, the Key editor is by far the most "musical" way of editing. That is, if you are familiar with a piano keyboard, with bars and beats, or with the basic operation of a tape recorder, then you'll find this editor to be the most user friendly when you take your first stab at MIDI editing. To say that the Key editor is the only editor you'll ever require, however, would be as silly as saying Cubase is the only program you'll ever need. Just as you could use a pair of scissors, a knife, a chainsaw, or a razor blade to cut a rope, you might use any one of Cubase's other MIDI editors to complete a task, but in a different way. As you master all of the many tools in the Key editor, you will find that you already know how to use the majority of the tools in Cubase's other MIDI editors.

You don't have to know how to play keyboards to use the Key editor, but it *is* important for you to realize that because Cubase was created with the musician in mind, having at least a basic understanding of music theory will *really* pay off. That's because, unlike software like Acid and

Reason—both great programs—Cubase forces you to create music from scratch, much the way an artist or writer is forced to start with a blank canvas or sheet of paper.

Of course, starting from scratch can be intimidating. To help you along, I've created a demo song using Cubase 4 and the virtual synths included in the program. You can use this song, included on the CD-ROM found at the back of this book, to follow along with me as I cover MIDI editing in the Key editor step by step.

To open the demo song, do the following:

1. With Cubase 4 running, insert the CD-ROM at the back of this book into your computer's CD-ROM drive.

2. In Cubase 4, open the File menu and choose Open.

3. Navigate to your computer's CD-ROM drive and double-click the icon for the Skill Pack CD-ROM to reveal the folders on the disc.

4. Double-click the Cubase Songs folder to open it.

5. Click the song titled Song1.

6. Click the Open button. Cubase loads Song1 (this may take a moment) along with all the virtual synths and their settings. When the song is loaded, it should look like the screen shown in Figure 1.1.

7. Click the Play button on the transport to play Song1; you'll see the cursor move across the screen from left to right.

Figure 1.1

The Key editor window, showing the MIDI bass part on my demo Song1.

> **NOTE**
>
> An alternative approach is to drag the CD-ROM's contents from the CD-ROM to your hard drive and work from your hard drive instead of the CD-ROM.

The Note Display and the Ruler

As you listen to Song1, notice how the cursor moves across the screen from left to right, passing little red boxes along the way. These boxes represent the MIDI notes being played by a synth bass, with the box located at the cursor representing the current note. If you can distinguish the bass part by ear, you can think of these little red boxes, which I'll call *notes* from now on, as visually representing the notes you hear. By watching the screen while listening to the song, you should be able to get a basic idea of where the bass part has been and where it's going.

The area that contains the notes is the *note display*, and the grid in this area indicates the pitch and duration of the notes on the screen. If you are familiar with a keyboard, you can use the visual keyboard reference on the left side of the screen to determine the pitch of the notes; if not, just recognize that the higher a note is on the screen, the higher its pitch. As for duration, it's indicated by the length of the red box that represents the note.

> **NOTE**
>
> If you are familiar with reading sheet music, you may be confused as to why Steinberg decided to use little red boxes and a grid to represent a part rather than quarter notes, eighth notes, and a staff. Doesn't it seem like they just reinvented the wheel? Yes . . . and no. I promise that in time, after you've spent some time using Cubase, Steinberg's decision to represent notation in this way will begin to make sense. I guarantee that you'll eventually realize how much more musical and simple Steinberg's method is compared to manuscript. Don't get me wrong: There's definitely a time and place for manuscript—but *not* when you're editing MIDI. In fact, I firmly believe that if Mozart were here today, even he would approve of Cubase's innovative method for editing MIDI.

Just above the note display, you'll see some numbers running sequentially from left to right, with little lines as spacers in between (see Figure 1.2). These numbers represent the *ruler*, which determines how you view the time reference to your MIDI part. You can adjust the ruler to display your part in bars and beats, seconds, timecode, or samples, or even customize the ruler to display time reference in the increments of your choice.

To do so, right-click anywhere on the ruler and click the desired setting in the pop-up menu that appears (here, Bars and Beats, because it is the most musical of the available options and is therefore best when working with MIDI). Notice that a checkmark appears next to the option you chose to indicate that it has been selected. Then, looking at the bass part for Song1, notice that the part starts at measure 9 and ends at measure 23, with each mark between the numbers in the ruler representing a beat in that measure. (Here, because the song is in 4/4 time, each measure is divided into 4 beats.)

Figure 1.2
The ruler.

> **NOTE**
>
> You may be wondering why you need so many ways to view time. Put simply, just as you sometimes need to measure something using a ruler but require a meter stick for other measurements, you may sometimes need to use different time references when working in Cubase. That said, when working with MIDI, I highly recommend you use bars and beats as your time reference. Cubase's real-time options exist primarily to accommodate screen composers and sound designers, who use the program to sync to video, or others who use time as a reference when syncing to analog tape machines.

The Toolbar

Located right above the ruler is the *toolbar* (see Figure 1.3), which houses most of the editing tools you'll use in each of the various MIDI editors (although there are subtle differences between the tools in each of the various MIDI editors). Because Cubase offers a number of tools—more than can fit across the screen in a single-monitor setup—you might want to customize the toolbar to hold only those tools you use most often. To add a tool to the toolbar, right-click anywhere on the toolbar and choose the tool from the pop-up menu that appears. Remove a tool that's already displayed by right-clicking the toolbar and clicking the tool in the menu.

Figure 1.3
The Cubase toolbar.

If you really want to get fancy with your toolbar setup, you can create presets for multiple tool setups (see Figure 1.4). This comes in especially handy when working with only one monitor, and allows you to quickly change from one style of editing to another. Alternatively, if you have the luxury of using a dual-monitor setup (which I highly recommend), you can display all the available tools rather than customizing the toolbar to display only a select few. To do so, stretch the Key editor across both monitors, right-click the toolbar, and choose Show All. If you will be working with only one monitor, you will need to adjust the view of the toolbar as we go over each tool.

NOTE

I go over all the available Cubase MIDI tools in Chapter 3, "The Toolbar."

Figure 1.4
The toolbar menu.

Zooming and Changing Views

As you start to get into editing, you'll find that knowing how to change your views within an editor so that you can give each individual note the attention it deserves is very important. The easiest—and often best—way to change the scope of your view is by using the Zoom control, located in the bottom-right area of your screen (see Figure 1.5).

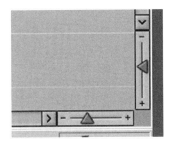

Figure 1.5
The Zoom control.

The Zoom control features two sliders: one positioned horizontally and one positioned vertically. To the left of the horizontal slider is a minus sign (–), and to the right of the same slider is a plus sign (·). If you click the minus sign, Cubase zooms your view out on the editor horizontally to display more bars and beats of the part you are working with. In contrast, clicking the plus sign by the horizontal slider zooms in on the editor horizontally, displaying fewer bars and beats of the part you are editing. When zooming horizontally, Cubase uses the curser as its point of reference; in other words, the location of your cursor determines the area of the screen that is reduced or expanded. For a more dramatic horizontal zoom, click and hold on the plus or minus button, or use your mouse to drag the slider between the two buttons. In addition to zooming horizontally, you can also zoom vertically using the plus and minus buttons alongside the vertical slider or by adjusting the slider itself; doing so affects the view of the grid with regard to pitch. (Note that unlike with the horizontal zoom, the vertical zoom feature does not zoom in and out from using the cursor as the point of reference; instead, it simply stretches or reduces the view.)

In addition to zooming in and out of the Key editor, you can adjust your view with the boxes across the bottom and along the right side of the screen (see Figure 1.6), known as *scroll bars*. By dragging the box along the bottom, you can change the view to display what's in front of or behind the grid's current contents. To focus on notes that are higher or lower in pitch, drag the box on the right side of the screen. (You'll use these controls throughout the book to adjust your view to match the illustrations shown.)

Figure 1.6
The horizontal view adjustment tool.

2 The Tool Buttons

T his chapter explores what many consider the most useful tools in Cubase: the tool buttons, which are located on the toolbar and grouped together. Cubase 4's Key editor contains 10 of these buttons (see Figure 2.1), each offering easy access to tools that play an important role in the editing process. (You'll learn about Cubase's other tool buttons in Chapter 3, "The Toolbar," after you master the 10 tools covered here.) Continue to follow along using Song1 from the CD-ROM, as you did in Chapter 1, "A Quick Look at the Key Editor."

Figure 2.1
The tool buttons.

You select any one of these 10 tools by clicking its tool button on the toolbar. When you do, the tool button changes to blue, and the cursor changes to reflect the tool you chose. Alternatively, you can select one of these tools from a special pop-up menu, or *tool box*. To do so, move the Object Selection tool (discussed in a moment) anywhere in the note display, right-click, and choose the desired tool from the pop-up menu that appears (see Figure 2.2). While I usually prefer to access Cubase's tools from the pop-up menu, you should do so in whichever way works best for you. Using any or all of these methods can help speed up and ease your work in Cubase.

Figure 2.2
The pop-up tool box.

The Object Selection Tool (OST)

The left-most tool button, which is marked by an arrow, is the Object Selection tool (OST) button (see Figure 2.3). You'll find that you use this tool more than any other tool in Cubase. In fact, along with your mouse, you will probably use this tool more than your computer keyboard and MIDI keyboard combined.

Figure 2.3
The OST button.

As you've already learned, the most basic use of the Object Selection tool is to select a note, object, or tool. You can also use the OST in the Key editor to play the keyboard on the left side of the screen; simply move the OST over the keys and click to hear a particular note. The OST will trigger the synth or sampler you have set up on the currently displayed track. In addition, the OST can be used to move notes or change the length of notes, either individually or as a group.

> **NOTE**
>
> Notice how the OST button appears blue. That's because it has already been selected; you used it to select notes.

Moving Notes

To use the OST to move a note in the note display, click the note with the OST and, while continuing to hold the mouse button down, move the OST to the desired location. Releasing the mouse button will finalize the move. (You'll find that you perform this type of operation, called *clicking and dragging*, quite often when editing in Cubase.)

To practice moving a note, do the following:

1. Click the OST button to select the OST.
2. In Song1, click the bass note at measure 13, beat 1 and hold the mouse button down.
3. With the mouse button still pressed, move the OST to the start of measure 15, beat 1.
4. Release the mouse button. The bass note is now located at the start of measure 15.Use Figure 2.4 to check your work.

In addition to moving a single note, you can move groups of notes. To do so, you must first use the OST to *select* the group of notes you want to move; Cubase surrounds the selected notes with a selection box, which you can resize as needed to select additional notes or de-select notes you don't want to move. Here's how it works:

8

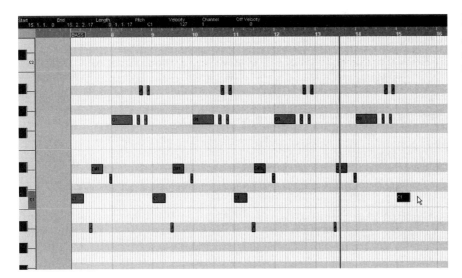

Figure 2.4
A note has been moved from measure 13 to measure 15.

1. Click the OST button to select the OST.

2. In Song1, place the OST at the start of measure 14, somewhere on the note display above the notes in the measure.

3. Click and drag the OST down and to the right until it is below the bottom notes just before measure 15. Cubase creates a selection box around the five notes in the measure (see Figure 2.5).

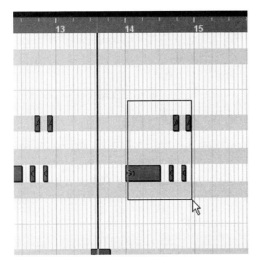

Figure 2.5
The OST multiple-object selection box.

4. Release the mouse button. Notice that the notes in the measure appear shaded; this indicates that they are selected.

5. Click and drag the first selected note from measure 14, beat 1 to measure 16, beat 1, keeping the note at its pitch position of G1.

6. Release the mouse button. The entire bass part is now located at measure 16 (see Figure 2.6).

7. Play the part back to hear the change.

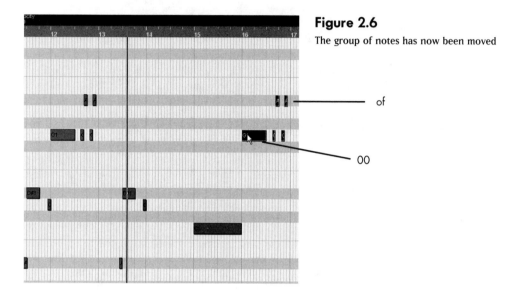

Figure 2.6

The group of notes has now been moved

of

00

If the process of selecting multiple objects with the OST seems a little clumsy at first, don't worry. After you've done it enough times, it will become as easy as clicking the mouse.

NOTE

The selection box created by the OST need not completely surround any object in order to select it. Even if part of a note is outside the selection box, Cubase will consider it selected.

Changing Note Lengths

In addition to using the OST to move notes, you can also use it to change the length of notes. To change the length of a single note, do the following:

1. Click the OST button to select the OST.

2. In Song1, using the OST, select the single bass note you moved in the preceding section from measure 13 to measure 15.

3. Position the OST along the right side of the bass note. A double-sided arrow will appear (see Figure 2.7).

Figure 2.7

Lengthening a note with the OST.

4. With the double arrow present, click and drag to the right until the edge of the note reaches measure 16.

5. Release the mouse button. Your bass note now stretches from measure 15 to measure 16 (see Figure 2.8).

6. Play the part back to hear the change.

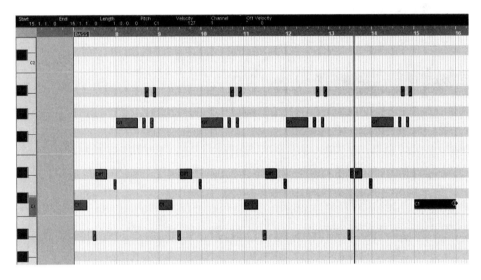

Figure 2.8

The lengthened note.

In addition to changing the length of a single note, you can also alter the lengths of multiple parts in one operation. Here's how:

1. Click the OST button to select the OST.

2. In Song1, position the OST at B1, just above the last two notes of measure 12.

3. Click and drag down and to the right to create a selection box around the last two A# notes of measure 12 (see Figure 2.9).

4. Release the mouse button. Both notes are selected.

5. Position the OST along the right side of the second note. A double-sided arrow appears (see Figure 2.10).

11

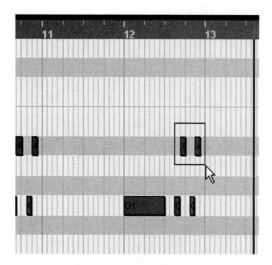

Figure 2.9
Selecting the notes with the OST.

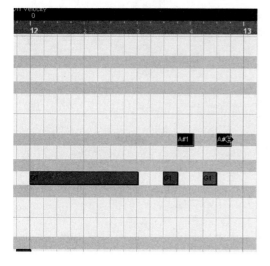

Figure 2.10
Lengthening multiple notes with the OST.

6. With the double arrow present, click and drag to the right until you reach bar 13.

7. Release the mouse button. As shown in Figure 2.11, both notes are now longer.

8. Play the part back to hear the change.

The Draw Tool

To the right of the OST button is the Draw tool button, which is marked with a small drawing of a pencil (see Figure 2.12). The main purpose of the Draw tool is to create an object that doesn't already exist in your song. Because you are working with the note display, the object you will be creating will be a note.

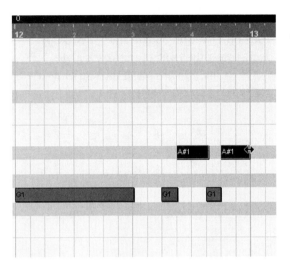

Figure 2.11
The selected notes have been lengthened.

Figure 2.12
The Draw tool button.

To create a note with the Draw tool, do the following:

1. Click the Draw tool button to select the Draw tool.

2. In Song1, position the Draw tool pointer, which looks like a pencil, at the start of measure 17 on note C1. (Use the keyboard on the left side of the screen as a guide for finding the correct pitch, and use the ruler to find the right measure or beat.)

3. Click the left mouse button. Congrats! You just created a new note (see Figure 2.13).

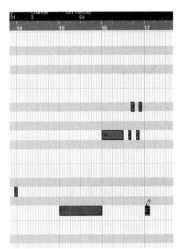

Figure 2.13
A new note.

In addition to using the Draw tool to create a note, you can also use it to lengthen the note in much the same way as with the OST. With the Draw tool, however, no double-sided arrow appears because you can drag in only one direction: to the right. To get the hang of this, click and drag the note with the Draw tool to extend the right edge of the note all the way to the end of measure 17 (see Figure 2.14).

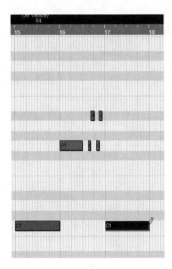

Figure 2.14

Lengthening a note with the Draw tool.

The Erase Tool

To the right of the Draw tool button is the Erase tool button, which features a drawing of a small eraser (see Figure 2.15). You use this tool to get rid of objects you no longer want in your project.

Figure 2.15

The Erase tool button.

To erase an unwanted object, simply click the object with the Erase tool. Alternatively, you can erase multiple objects at once by doing the following:

1. Click the Erase tool button to select the Erase tool.

2. In Song1, position the Erase tool pointer, which looks like an eraser, at measure 13 such that it is higher than the notes in the measure.

3. Click and drag the Erase tool down and to the right to create a selection box that covers the three notes in measure 13, as shown in Figure 2.16.

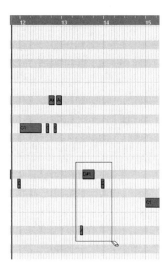

Figure 2.16
Selecting notes with the Erase tool.

4. Release the mouse button.

5. Click any one of the three notes selected; all three notes disappear (see Figure 2.17).

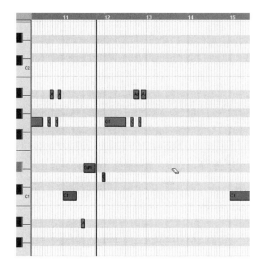

Figure 2.17
Poof! The notes are gone.

The Mute Tool

To the right of the Erase tool button is the Mute tool button (see Figure 2.18), symbolized by an × symbol. The Mute tool works similarly to the Erase tool, but instead of erasing unwanted objects, it simply mutes them, or prevents them from being heard; when you're ready to listen to a muted note again, you can un-mute it.

Figure 2.18
The Mute tool button.

Here's an exercise to walk you through using the Mute tool.

1. Click the Mute tool button to select the Mute tool.

2. In Song1, position the Mute tool pointer, which looks like a small ×, on the bass note you created between measures 17 and 18 and click to select the note. As shown in Figure 2.19, the note changes from red to white, indicating that the note is muted.

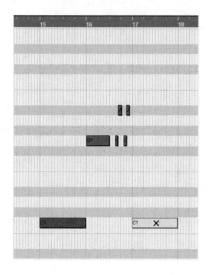

Figure 2.19
A muted note.

3. Play back the track to confirm that the note is muted.

4. Click the muted note a second time to un-mute it, bringing it back to its original state.

To mute (and un-mute) multiple notes at once, use the click-and-drag method to create a selection box around the multiple notes and click any of the selected notes with the Mute tool to perform the operation.

The Trim Tool

To the right of the Mute tool button is a button for a tool that is relatively new to Cubase: the Trim tool. As shown in Figure 2.20, the Trim tool button features a small graphic of a knife. The Trim tool enables you to act like a MIDI surgeon, editing MIDI note lengths.

Figure 2.20

The Trim tool button.

You can use the Trim tool on a single note or on multiple notes. Here's how:

1. Click the Trim tool button to select the Trim tool.

2. In Song1, position the Trim tool pointer, which looks like a small knife, on the middle of the note between measures 15 and 16 and click (see Figure 2.21). The note is trimmed into half its original length, as shown in Figure 2.22.

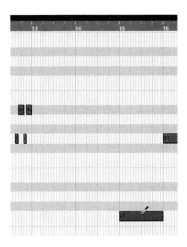

Figure 2.21

Preparing to trim the note.

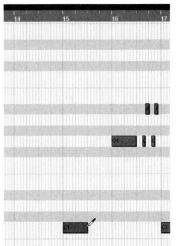

Figure 2.22

The note is trimmed.

3. Position the Trim tool above and toward the middle of the first note in measure 12, as shown in Figure 2.23.

4. Click and drag the pointer down and to the left until it's just below the middle of the first note in measure 11. With the mouse button still pressed, notice that the Trim tool has created a line from your starting point to the tool's current location; use this line as a guide to help you choose the Trim tool's path (see Figure 2.24). When you release the mouse button, the right-most portions of the objects in the Trim tool's path will be trimmed according to the position of this guide line.

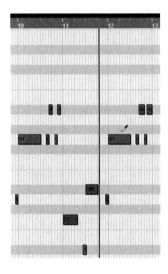

Figure 2.23
Positioning the Trim tool.

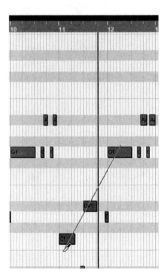

Figure 2.24
Positioning the Trim guideline.

5. Release the mouse button. The three notes in the Trim tool's path are trimmed, as shown in Figure 2.25.

6. Play back the track to hear the change.

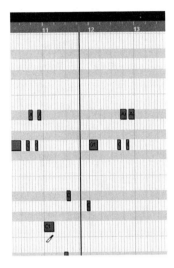

Figure 2.25

Three notes are trimmed at once.

The Split Tool

To the right of the Trim tool button is the Split tool button, which features a pair of scissors (see Figure 2.26). You use this tool to divide, or split, one object into two separate objects. When you use this tool, it actually creates a new start point for the new note to the right of the tool's position. With the note split in two, you can edit the pitch, velocity, length, and start and end times of each part separately.

Figure 2.26

The Split tool button.

To get a handle on using the Split tool, let's use a different demo song: Song2. First, close Song1 by clicking the X button in the top-right corner of the Key editor and the project window, optionally saving your changes to the Song1 file to your hard drive. Next, open Song2 on the CD-ROM by following the steps in Chapter 1. Then do the following:

1. Click the Split tool button to select the Split tool.

2. In Song2, locate the long string note held between measures 14 and 19.

3. Position the Split tool pointer, which looks like a tiny pair of scissors, so the tip is on the note at measure 15, beat 1, as shown in Figure 2.27, and click. The note is split at measure 15, as indicated by a line (see Figure 2.28).

19

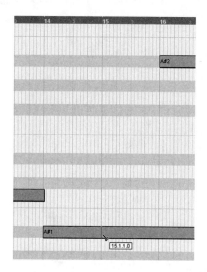

Figure 2.27

Positioning the Split tool.

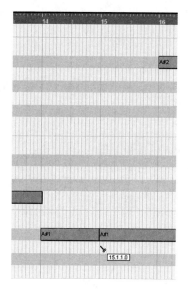

Figure 2.28

The note is split.

4. Play back the track, listening as the cursor moves past the split point. You will hear the note stop and then start at measure 15 instead of being one long note.

In addition to enabling you to split a single note, you can also use the Split tool to split multiple notes at once. Here's how:

1. Starting with the Split tool pointer over the top note at measure 17, click and drag down and to the right until the cursor is below the bottom note at measure 18, as shown in Figure 2.29.

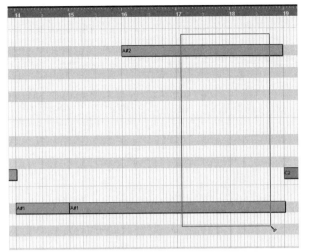

Figure 2.29
Selecting multiple notes with the Split tool.

2. Release the mouse button. Two notes are now selected in their entirety.

3. To split the top note at measure 18, click the note at measure 18, beat 1 (see Figure 2.30). Each of the two notes is split, forming a total of four notes.

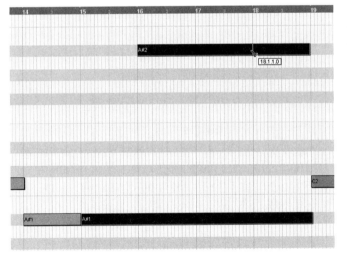

Figure 2.30
Positioning the Split tool to split multiple notes.

4. Click the Erase tool button.

5. Click the two newly created notes that start at measure 18 to erase them. This alters the end points and lengths of the original string part, as shown in Figure 2.31.

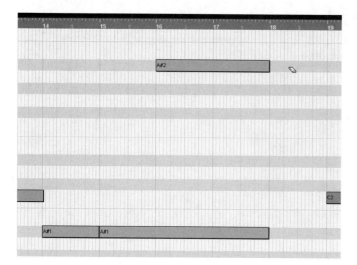

Figure 2.31

Poof! The second half of both notes is gone.

The Glue Tool

To the right of the Split tool button is the Glue tool button, which features what I can only assume is supposed to be a stick or bottle of glue (see Figure 2.32). This tool goes hand in hand with the Split tool but works in the opposite way, enabling you to fuse two separate objects into one.

Figure 2.32

The Glue tool button.

To use the Glue tool, do the following:

1. Click the Glue tool button to select the Glue tool.

2. In Song2, position the Glue tool pointer, which looks like a small bottle of glue, so that it's anywhere on the note at measure 14 (see Figure 2.33) and click. The note that was to the right of the pointer merges with the note you just clicked; put another way, the notes have been "glued together" to form one long note (see Figure 2.34).

> **NOTE**
>
> When using the Glue tool, avoid over clicking. Each click with the Glue tool glues the note you click to the following note. Too many clicks can lead to a messy, gooey blob, and nobody wants that.

> **NOTE**
>
> Even if there is a space between the note you click and the note to the right, the Glue tool fills the gap to connect the two notes.

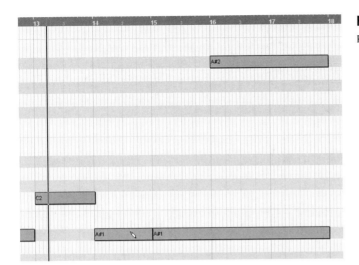

Figure 2.33
Preparing to glue.

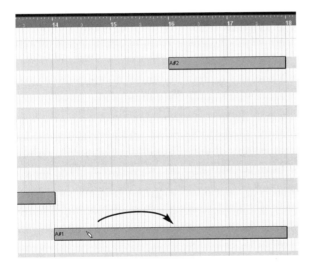

Figure 2.34
The newly glued note.

In addition to using the Glue tool to glue two notes, the tool can be used to glue multiple sets of notes, but doing so can be a little tricky. Here's an example:

1. Position the Glue tool pointer at the start of measure 7 at E2, click, and drag down and to the right until the Glue tool is positioned at C2, just before the start of measure 8 (see Figure 2.35).

2. Release the mouse button.

3. With the two notes selected, position the Glue tool pointer on the top note and click; the Glue tool fills the gap between both the top and bottom selected notes and the notes to their right side, gluing them together (see Figure 2.36).

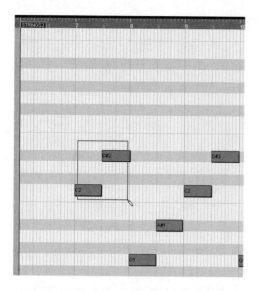

Figure 2.35

Selecting notes with the Glue tool.

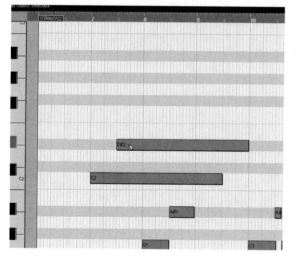

Figure 2.36

Filling the gaps with glue between two notes.

4. Here's where things can get messy. Repeat step 1 to select the two newly combined notes.

5. Position the Glue tool pointer on the top note and click. Because each of these notes had neighboring notes that started at different times, the new notes have separate lengths (see Figure 2.37). If you play this back, you'll notice that it doesn't sound very nice.

6. Click the Erase tool button.

7. Using the Erase tool, select and erase everything between measure 7 at E2 and measure 18 at F1.

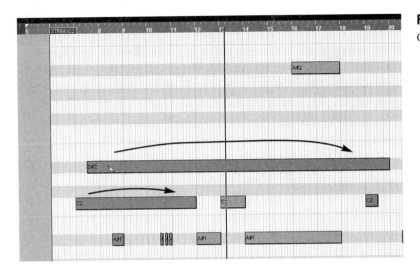

Figure 2.37

Oops! I spilled the glue!

The Zoom Tool

Located to the right of the Glue tool button is the Zoom tool button, which features a magnifying glass (see Figure 2.38). This tool does the same basic thing as the Zoom control in the bottom-right corner of the Key editor, but in a slightly different way. Specifically, it enables you to target the exact area you want to zoom in or out on.

Figure 2.38

The Zoom tool button.

To operate the Zoom tool, do the following:

1. Click the Zoom tool button to select the Zoom tool.

2. In Song2, position the Zoom tool pointer, which looks like a cross-hair, over the area of the screen you want to zoom in on and click.

3. To take an even closer look, click again, repeating as needed until you have achieved the desired zoom level.

4. To zoom out, position the pointer over the area of the screen you want to zoom out of and click the mouse while pressing the Alt key on your Windows keyboard or pressing the Option key on your Mac keyboard (also referred to as *Alt-clicking* or *Option-clicking*).

To zoom in on a group of notes, first click and drag the Zoom tool to create a selection box around the notes you want to include. When you release the button, Cubase zooms in on the selected notes. (Note that zooming out on a group of notes is achieved the same way you zoom out on a single note, as described earlier in this chapter.)

The Line Tool

The Line tool button, which features a diagonal line, is located to the right of the Zoom tool button on the toolbar (see Figure 2.39). Unlike the tools you've seen so far, clicking the small arrow in the bottom-right corner of this toolbar button reveals a drop-down menu, from which you can select one of six line types. (Note that this arrow appears only on the toolbar button, not in the pop-up menu discussed earlier in the chapter.) You might use this tool to create a line in the note display, which is useful for creating an ascending or descending flourish of notes.

Figure 2.39
The Line tool button and drop-down menu.

NOTE

For now, I'm going to skip going into detail about the Line tool; there are a few other things you need to learn first. You'll learn more about this tool in Chapter 4: "The Controller Lanes and the Line Tool."

The Time Warp Tool

The Time Warp tool button, which, inexplicably, features what appears to be a row of boxes of different widths (rather than, say, a clock), is the last in the group of these 10 tool buttons (see Figure 2.40). You use this tool, which is relatively new to Cubase, to create tempo changes in a song when using real time–based audio and MIDI recordings. Because this tool has more to do with tempo-map editing and real audio than with MIDI, I won't be getting into it in any more detail.

Figure 2.40
The Time Warp tool button.

3 The Toolbar

Having learned how to use the 10 key tool buttons discussed in Chapter 2, "The Tool Buttons," you're ready to discover the rest of the buttons on the Key editor's toolbar. In this chapter, you'll explore these buttons, starting in the top-left area of the toolbar and working across from left to right. (Remember: If you can't find one of the buttons discussed in this chapter, it's probably because that button is not currently displayed. Simply display the remaining tools on the toolbar as discussed at the end of Chapter 1, "A Quick Look at the Key Editor.") As with the tool buttons discussed in Chapter 2, these tool buttons appear blue in color when selected.

> **NOTE**
>
> Before you move forward, take a moment to close any songs you may have open in Cubase and load Song1. (For details on how to load Song1, refer to Chapter 1.)

The Solo Editing Button

A few tool buttons are always present on the toolbar by default. One such tool button is the Solo Editing button, which is located in the top-left area of the toolbar and features a capital letter S with a lowercase e (see Figure 3.1). When you play back a part while the Solo Editing button is activated, only the track selected in the Key editor will play. This makes it much easier to concentrate on the part you are currently working on and offers an extremely easy way to toggle back and forth between hearing that single track and hearing the entire mix.

To use this feature, do the following:

1. With Song1 open, click the Solo Editing button to activate the feature. (The color of the button will change to blue.)

Figure 3.1

The Solo Editing button

2. Click Play on the transport; only the bass track plays back.

3. Click the Solo Editing button to toggle this feature off.

4. Click Play on the transport again; this time, all the tracks play.

The Acoustic Feedback Button

The Acoustic Feedback button is to the right of the Solo Editing button; it features a speaker that appears to be blasting music (see Figure 3.2). Simply put, this tool enables you to hear the note you are working with as it is created or when it is selected—very handy when you want to hear how an edit has affected the note you are working with.

Figure 3.2

The Acoustic Feedback button.

To use this feature, do the following:

1. With Song1 open, click the Acoustic Feedback button to activate the feature. (The color of the button will change to blue.)

2. Click the Object Selection button to select the Object Selection tool.

3. Click a note in the bass part. You'll hear the note play.

4. Repeat step 3 with several notes. As you do, you'll hear the various pitches of the bass track.

> **NOTE**
>
> You may be wondering why you would ever disable the Acoustic Feedback tool. One scenario might be if you are engaged in a lot of repetitive editing and you don't need to hear the result every time; disabling Cubase's Acoustic Feedback tool might make your work more pleasant. More importantly, you won't annoy your neighbors as much. For now, however, don't worry about your neighbors; leave Acoustic Feedback on as you work so you can hear what you're doing to the notes.

The Show Info Line Button

The Show Info Line button, to the right of the Acoustic Feedback button, features a rectangular box with a downward-pointing arrow (see Figure 3.3). When you click this button, a bar of information, called the *Info Line*, opens up between the toolbar and the ruler, as shown in Figure 3.4.

This Info Line displays information about the selected MIDI note, including seven editable parameters: Note Start Time, Note End Time, Note Length, Pitch, Velocity, MIDI Channel, and Off Velocity. For example, to view these parameters for the first note in the bass part, click the note. If you select a different note in the sequence, these values will change accordingly. To change what information appears in the Info Line, right-click it; a pop-up menu appears, enabling you to select the information you want to display (see Figure 3.5).

Figure 3.3

The Show Info Line button.

Figure 3.4

The Info Line.

Figure 3.5

The Info Line menu.

The Note Start, Note End, and Note Length Parameters

The values in the Note Start, Note End, and Note Length parameters in the Info Line indicate the position of the selected note within the Note display grid with respect to the ruler. Whether the ruler is set to display time in bars and beats or in seconds determines what specific information is displayed in these parameters.

In your case, because your ruler is set to bars and beats, when you look at the Note Start field for the first bass note in your bass part, you can see that the part starts at 7.1.1.0. This means the bass note is played at measure 7, on beat 1. The Note End field shows that the note ends at 7.2.1.17, meaning that it ends slightly after measure 7, beat 2. (The decimal places to the right of the second decimal point represent finer divisions of another beat, down to the exact ending point.) If either the start note or end note value is adjusted, the Note Length value will automatically change to match the new settings. If the Note Length value is changed, only the Note End value is adjusted to match the new length.

To adjust any of these values, simply click on the decimal place of the value you'd like to change and manually type a new value using your computer keyboard. Alternatively, if your mouse has a wheel, click the decimal place you want to change and use the wheel to scroll up or down until you find the value you want. You can also use the up and down arrows on your keyboard to adjust these settings. Experiment by changing the length of the first bass note to 0.1.1.0 (that is, changing the value in the last decimal place from .17 to .0); notice how, when you change this value, the Note End value changes to match. (Of course, this change will be almost inaudible during playback.)

You might adjust these settings in order to shorten the slight overhangs of note lengths that sometimes occur with mono synths or if you're programming an instrument that is normally played in mono (i.e., a solo flute or a trumpet), and the next note starts before the overhang ends, resulting in an unflattering effect. For an audible solution, try changing the start time to 7.2.1.0 and the length to 0.0.2.0; when you play back the track, you should be able to hear that the groove has changed, with the bass now starting on beat two instead of beat one. (After you listen to the changes, reset the altered bass note's start time to 7.1.1.0 and its length to 0.1.0.0.)

The Note Pitch Parameter

The Info Line's Note Pitch field reveals the pitch of the selected note. For example, the Note Pitch parameter of the bass note you've been working with indicates that the note is at C1, which means the pitch of the note is C in the first octave. To alter the pitch of the note using the Info Line, simply use the same method you used to adjust the note start and note end times: Click the pitch you want to change and type a new value, or use the mouse wheel or the up and down arrows on your keyboard to scroll to the desired pitch. Here, try changing the note's pitch from C1 to C2 on the Info Line. When you play back the note, you should be able to hear that it is in fact one octave higher in pitch; likewise, looking at the grid, you will see that it has moved up exactly one octave.

The Note Velocity Parameter

The Info Line's Note Velocity parameter enables you to adjust how *hard* the selected note is played or struck. (This sometimes, but not always, affects how loudly a note is played.) Most of the time, adjusting the velocity of a note results in subtle differences in the timbre or tonality of the sound, although the settings within the synth or sampler are also a factor in how the note sounds with certain velocity settings applied.

In this example, the Note Velocity value for the first note in your bass part is at the highest setting, 127. If you change this value from 127 to 10 (again, using your keyboard, mouse wheel, or arrow keys) and listen to the track, you should hear a subtle difference in the tonality of the bass. Specifically, when the setting was at 127, the bass tone had more of a bite, or harshness, to it; lowering the velocity results in a softer attack than before, as if you were playing gently on a keyboard instead of banging on the keys.

The Note MIDI Channel Setting

The Note MIDI Channel setting enables you to change the MIDI playback channel for the selected note. You can select MIDI channel 1–16 using the same technique you used to alter the length, pitch, velocity, and other settings (that is, using your keyboard, mouse wheel, or arrow keys); your MIDI output is determined by the output settings defined on your track.

Chances are, you'd change this setting only when performing some tricky playback stunts. For example, if you were working with a sequenced guitar part and you wanted to trigger a guitar squeal or screech from your sampler when you hit a particular note, you could assign a squeal sound to MIDI channel 16 on another synth and then adjust that particular note to playback on channel 16. When you played back your part, the other notes would play as normal, but the note you changed would play back the sound of a guitar squeal. This could be used to create some complex sound textures.

The Off Velocity Setting

If *velocity* refers to how hard the selected note is played or struck, then *off velocity* describes how hard the note sounds at the instant you stop playing the note. If you're having trouble grasping this, consider that just because *you've* stopped playing a note doesn't mean that your synth can't continue to play it without you. For example, you might have a sustain after a note stops, or a note might trigger a sample that has an endless loop. When you adjust this setting, you essentially tell your synth or sampler how hard you want it to play the sustained or held note.

In truth, most synths aren't programmed with Off Velocity settings; if you really want to dig into this setting, you may have to dig into your synth as well. For this reason, like the Note MIDI Channel setting, needing to change the MIDI Off Velocity setting is something of a rarity. Although there isn't currently a high demand for this MIDI parameter, Cubase included it so that maybe, someday, you could put it to good use.

> **NOTE**
>
> As you explore the world of MIDI editing, you will discover that there are many ways to make a similar edit. For example, although the numerical approach supported by the Info Line can be very useful for fine adjustments, using this tool can become tedious when editing on a larger scale. Think of the Info Line as a tool for microsurgical MIDI editing, where you can really hit the nail on the head when making detailed MIDI edits.

The Auto Scroll Button

The next group of toolbar buttons is composed of those tool buttons discussed in Chapter 2. If you have not yet made yourself familiar with these buttons, refer to Chapter 2 before moving forward.

Beyond the tool buttons, still moving from left to right across the toolbar, is the Auto Scroll button, which features an arrow pointing to the right with a vertical line passing through the middle (see Figure 3.6).

Figure 3.6

The Auto Scroll button.

By default, when you play a track, your view stays constant. The notes are stationary, and the cursor passes across the screen, showing only the portion of the track you are viewing. This works well if you're working on one small part of a track, but if you're working on a large section, you might want to see more. One option is to zoom out on your track to view more of it; alternatively, you can activate the Auto Scroll button.

When Auto Scroll is activated, the view "chases" the cursor. That is, as the cursor travels across the song, the screen is continuously updated to reveal both where the cursor is going and where it has just been. This is very helpful when dealing with a large section of music where the view is zoomed in because it helps speed the editing process.

The Auto Select Controllers Button

To the right of the Auto Scroll button is the Auto Select Controllers button, marked with an odd pyramid-type icon (see Figure 3.7). You'll learn more about this feature a bit later on in this chapter, in the section titled "Editing in a Controller Lane."

Figure 3.7

The Auto Select Controllers button.

> **NOTE**
>
> If you're wondering what the heck a controller is, here's a definition to help you out: A controller is used to perform any one of the 128 different actions that can be taken with a MIDI note. Some common controllers include modulation, velocity, aftertouch, sustain, volume, pan, pitchbend, and system exclusive, which you'll get into later in this book. If you're an average MIDI Joe, you'll probably use 10 of these controllers at most; beyond that, things start getting pretty technical. (Note that this term is confusing in that your MIDI keyboard is sometimes referred to as a *controller*. When you're editing MIDI, however, the term usually refers to these various MIDI functions.

The Show Part Borders Button, the Edit Active Part Only Button, and the Part List

Still working from left to right across the toolbar, the next set of tools, which includes the Show Part Borders button, the Edit Active Part Only button, and the Part List, is designed to work together.

- **The Show Part Borders button.** Like the Auto Scroll button, the Show Part Borders button, marked with an image that resembles a pair of flags and shown in Figure 3.8, is used to alter the display. Specifically, clicking this button focuses the view on the part you're working with instead of on the song as a whole.

Figure 3.8
The Show Part Borders button.

> **NOTE**
>
> A *part* is a subdivision of a track. You decide how long your parts are; a part might be an entire bass track or perhaps just a few notes in the track. If the parts in your song are the entire length of the song, clicking the Show Parts Border button will have little effect on your display. If, however, your parts are only a few measures in length, then clicking the Show Parts Borders button will limit the display to the part you're working on, from start to finish.

- **The Edit Active Part Only button.** To the right of the Show Part Borders button is the Edit Active Part Only button, marked with a cursive lowercase e and an exclamation point (see Figure 3.9). When this button is activated, Cubase enables you to edit only the selected part. For instance, suppose you want to view an entire track, but the part that you want to edit is only two measures long. With the Edit Active Part Only button activated, and with the Show Part Borders button *de*-activated, you will be able to see the entire track, but you will be unable to modify notes outside the selected part. In a way, this is a safety feature, designed to prevent you from changing things accidentally. You'll learn more about this feature in Appendix A, "Working with Multiple MIDI Tracks in an Editor."

Figure 3.9
The Edit Active Part Only button.

- **The Part List.** Next to the Edit Active Part Only button is the Part List (see Figure 3.10), which is another tool for changing views while editing. For example, if you want to work with multiple parts at once, you can use the Part List—basically a drop-down list that contains the parts you have selected—to easily change your view from part to part. (Note that generally speaking, you select parts from the project window, which I will discuss in detail in Chapter 6, "Working with MIDI in the Project Window.") The Part List works well when used in conjunction with the Show Part Borders button if you're working with several parts at once that are located next to each other, as well as if you're working with multiple tracks in the Key editor. You'll learn more about the Part List in Appendix A.

Figure 3.10

The Part List.

The Insert Velocity Display

Next to the Part List is another drop-down list—this one called the Insert Velocity display and marked with numbers and the abbreviation "ins. vel." (see Figure 3.11). The value displayed here defines the default velocity of any note that is created using the tools within Cubase. For example, if you create a note in Cubase using the Draw tool, and the Insert Velocity is set to 100, then the velocity strength of the note you just created is 100 by default. In contrast, if you were to create the same note by pressing its key on a MIDI keyboard rather than by using one of the tools in Cubase, the note's velocity value would depend on how hard you hit the key.

Figure 3.11

The Insert Velocity parameter.

You have several options for changing the settings of the Insert Velocity parameter:

- ■ Click the displayed value to select it and use your computer keyboard to enter a new value, pressing Enter to make the velocity change.

- ■ Click the up and down arrows to the right of the Insert Velocity display. This enables you to scroll upward or downward through the available values one digit at a time and is especially handy for small changes.

- ■ Use a preset velocity setting. These are stored in the Insert Velocity display's drop-down list, accessible via the arrow located in bottom-left corner of the Insert Velocity display. Select any one of the five available settings; the Insert Velocity display will change accordingly. (If none of the settings are appropriate, choose Setup from the drop-down menu and modify the available settings to better suit your needs.)

The Nudge Buttons

The next group of buttons—10 in all—is referred to as the *nudge buttons* (see Figure 3.12). These buttons, each featuring arrows pointing in various directions, provide a very useful way to move and change the lengths of notes in the Note display. (Note that to make it easier for you to keep track of which is which, I refer to these buttons by numbers 1–10 as they are positioned on the toolbar from left to right.)

Figure 3.12
The nudge buttons.

The last four buttons in the group—buttons 7–10—are great for moving the pitch of a note up or down. To get a handle on how these buttons work, try the following:

1. In Song1, using the OST, select the note located at measure 21, beat 1. This note should be C1.

2. With the note selected, click the seventh nudge button—the one with a small upward-pointing arrow. This moves the note up one half step.

3. Click the eighth nudge button, which features a small downward-pointing arrow to move the note back down one half step to its original position.

4. Notice how the next two nudge buttons feature slightly longer arrows. That's because they are used to nudge notes upward or downward in pitch in full-octave increments rather than half-note increments. To demonstrate, click the ninth nudge button (the one with the longer upward arrow); the note jumps from C1 to C2.

5. Change the note back from C2 to C1 by clicking the 10th nudge button, with the longer downward-pointing arrow.

As you probably noticed, using these buttons can be a very efficient way to move notes around in the Note display. But what about the first six nudge buttons?

- Buttons 1 and 2 are used to change the start location of the note and use the Quantize setting as a reference for the available increments.

- Buttons 3 and 4 are used to move the note left or right in the Note display. Like buttons 1 and 2, these buttons use the Quantize setting as a reference for the available increments.

- Buttons 5 and 6 are used to adjust the length of a note. They refer to the Length Q setting to determine the available increments.

Since I haven't gone over Quantize or Length Q settings yet, you'll learn more about these first six nudge buttons in the next few sections as I cover the Snap function and its controls.

The Snap Function Button, Snap Type Display, the Quantize Setting, and the Length Q Setting

The next four tools accessible via the toolbar are very important: They help you define the length of created notes as well as where the notes go when they are moved within the Note display. These tools are as follows.

The Snap Function Button

When the Snap Function button, shown in Figure 3.13, is activated, any notes you move or nudge will automatically snap to the closest grid point (which is defined in the Quantize display). In essence, enabling the Snap Function button magnetizes the grid such that when a note falls outside of the grid, the grid pulls it back in to stick to the closest grid line.

Figure 3.13

The Snap Function button.

> **NOTE**
>
> If you enter notes using a MIDI keyboard, you may find that the notes don't always fall directly on the grid (or, put another way, on beat). Even if a take sounded great to your human ear, when you examine it in the Note display, you may notice that a few of the notes you played are slightly out of time. Just because this performance doesn't *look* perfect, however, doesn't mean that it isn't. Only you can decide what's right or wrong.

The Snap Type Display

There are several ways to control Snap settings; one is by selecting the type of snap editing that will best suit your needs for the edit you're attempting to accomplish. You do this by clicking the Snap Type display, located to the right of the Snap Function button, and choosing the desired setting from the drop-down menu that appears (see Figure 3.14). Note that the graphic that appears in the Snap Type display changes according to which of the eight available snap types you choose (you'll explore these options further in a moment, in the section titled "Snapping, Nudging, Swapping, and Playing with Magnets"):

Figure 3.14

The Snap Type display and drop-down menu.

■ **Snap to Grid.** The Grid snap type, indicated by lines crossing to form a grid (see Figure 3.15), is the most common and the default snap type. When this snap type is used, objects are moved to the nearest line in the grid according to the settings established in the Quantize display (you'll learn about the Quantize setting in a moment). This snap type is great for ensuring that notes are directly on beat.

Figure 3.15

The Grid snap type.

■ **Snap to Grid Relative.** Suppose you like the fact that a note falls a little before or after a beat, but you need to move it to the next measure. The Grid Relative snap type, represented by a grid with a box in the middle (see Figure 3.16), is designed to move a note that doesn't fall on a beat such that the snap movement doesn't affect the natural placement of the note. It does this by calculating how far your note is from the grid in its initial position and then using that same calculation to place the note accordingly on the next grid when the note is moved. This is an excellent way to maintain a slightly off-beat note's position while moving notes around in the Note display.

Figure 3.16

The Grid Relative snap type.

■ **Snap to Events.** In some cases, you may not want a note or *event* (a fancy way of saying "anything recorded with MIDI") to be moved according to the grid at all. Instead, you might want to snap a note or event to another note or event, an option made possible by the Events snap type (see Figure 3.17). When you do, the snapped notes become magnetized to each other, sticking together when one or the other is moved. You might use this snap type if, for example, you wanted one note to start as soon as another note ended. If the first note doesn't end on a beat, this is one way to get the next note to fall directly after it.

Figure 3.17

The Events snap type.

NOTE

Using this snap type can be messy if you aren't careful; to help prevent a MIDI pile-up, Cubase still snaps to the grid at measures.

■ **Shuffle Snap.** This snap type, represented by a symbol similar to the one for "recycle" (see Figure 3.18), works a little differently than the rest. Suppose you have two notes that are side by side in the Note display, but you want to switch their order such that the second note precedes the first one. To do so, select this snap type; then drag the first note past the second note. The notes will swap places. You probably won't use this snap type very often, but you'll be glad you have it when you need it.

Figure 3.18

The Shuffle snap type.

■ **Snap to Magnetic Cursor.** Suppose you want to assemble several notes, all starting or stopping at the same place, and that place doesn't fall on a beat. To ensure that the notes fall correctly, try using the Magnetic Cursor snap type. When you select this snap type, represented by a horseshoe-shaped magnet pointing toward a vertical line (see Figure 3.19), everything that's moved toward the cursor's position will be positioned at the cursor's exact location on the timeline—very handy when you're trying to create an offbeat punch with several parts or notes playing at once.

Figure 3.19

The Magnetic Cursor snap type.

■ **The crazy snap combos.** If your need for snap goes beyond what you've learned so far, then you're *snap crazy!* The good news is that Cubase accommodates you by offering three combination snap types: Grid + Cursor, Events + Cursor, and Events + Grid + Cursor. As you probably guessed, each of these variations simply twists two or three different snap types together. Play around with these snap types to get a handle on how they work.

The Quantize Display

The *American Heritage Dictionary* defines the word *quantize* as "To limit the possible values of (a magnitude or quantity) to a discrete set of values by quantum mechanical rules." In my words, to quantize is to define the increments (in terms of beats) by which your MIDI events should be automatically aligned to your magnetic musical grid.

> **NOTE**
>
> In order to quantize in Cubase, you must set your ruler to display time in bars and beats. Cubase does not currently support quantization in terms of real time.

The toolbar's Quantize display, shown in Figure 3.20, includes a fairly simple drop-down list containing all sorts of options for defining your quantize increment. A Quantize setting of 1/1 limits you to moving your objects to the downbeat of every measure. In contrast, a Quantize setting of

½ limits you to moving your objects to the first and third beat of every measure. As you continue down the menu, the increments get smaller and smaller, finishing with triplet and dotted quantize types, which is helpful when working with notes that need to be quantized to a grid in a way other than the default straight time feel.

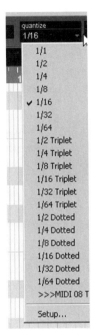

Figure 3.20

The Quantize display and menu.

For many types of music, establishing the correct Quantize setting is very important; otherwise, your groove will not be right. Note, too, that in many cases, you may need to alternate settings— say, from a regular time setting to a triplet or dotted setting—in order to acquire the correct groove. Again, knowing a little about music theory and rhythmic theory will help you decide which setting to use.

NOTE

Cubase also allows you to create your own templates for quantizing. You'll learn more about this—and other aspects of quantizing—in Chapter 8, "A Closer Look at Quantizing MIDI."

The Length Q Display

The Length Q display, located next to the Quantize display, is similar to the Quantize display (see Figure 3.21)—but instead of using it to define the increments for *moving* your notes on the grid, the Length Q display's drop-down menu is used to define the increments by which you *lengthen* your notes (for example, in quarter-note increments, eighth-note increments, half-note increments, and so on). The drop-down menu also includes a Quantize Link entry, which enables you to duplicate the setting of your Length Q to the current Quantize setting.

Figure 3.21

The Length Q display and menu.

Snapping, Nudging, Swapping, and Playing with Magnets

Oh snap! Get ready to quantize! The following exercise is long and covers a lot of things you've learned so far in this chapter:

1. In Song1, use your mouse to change the Quantize setting to $\frac{1}{4}$ and the Length Q setting to $\frac{1}{8}$.

2. Set the snap type to Grid.

3. If it's not activated already, activate the Snap Function button (see Figure 3.22).

4. Using the OST, move the first note in measure 9 to beat 2. Notice how you can't put it between beat 1 and beat 2; this is because the Quantize is set to $\frac{1}{4}$, which divides the measure into four equal parts (see Figure 3.23).

5. Shorten the first note by clicking and dragging the note to the left until it's halfway between beats 2 and 3, on the "and" of beat 2. Notice that you can shorten the note

40

between the grid lines because your Length Q setting is ⅛, which divides the measure into eight equal parts. Compare your work to what's shown in Figure 3.24 to make sure you're on the same page.

Figure 3.22
Establishing your settings.

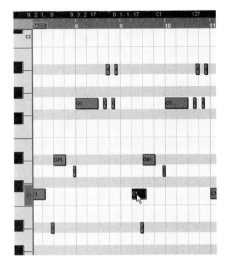

Figure 3.23
Moving the note.

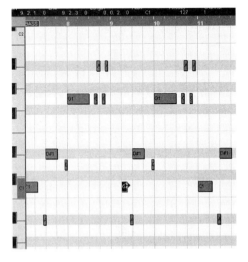

Figure 3.24
Note shortened to eighth-note length.

6. Change your Quantize setting to ⅛ and your Length Q to 1/16.

7. Using the OST, move the first bass note in measure 9 to the "and" of beat 1 in the measure, placing it between beats 1 and 2.

8. With the OST, click and drag the note to the left to shorten it by an increment of $\frac{1}{16}$. Notice how the new Quantize and Length Q settings have changed the way you can control the placement and sizing of the note. Compare your work to what's shown in Figure 3.25 to make sure you're still on track.

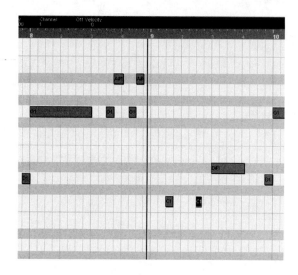

Figure 3.25

The altered note after step 7.

9. Change the Quantize setting to $\frac{1}{16}$ and select the second bass note in measure 9 (A#0).

10. Click the third nudge button (the one with the arrow pointing to the left) one time.

11. Click the seventh nudge button (the one with the small arrow pointing up) two times.

12. Change the Length Q setting to $\frac{1}{32}$.

13. Click the fifth nudge button one time, noticing how this adjusts the length. Compare your progress with what's shown in Figure 3.26 to double-check your work.

14. Change the Quantize setting to $\frac{1}{2}$.

15. Change the snap type to Grid Relative (see Figure 3.27).

16. Using the OST, select the last note in measure 11 (see Figure 3.28).

17. Click the fourth nudge button (the one with the arrow that points to the right) one time to move the note to the middle of measure 12. Notice that because the snap type is Grid Relative, the note keeps its place in relation to the grid (see Figure 3.29).

18. Select the G1 that starts at measure 12.

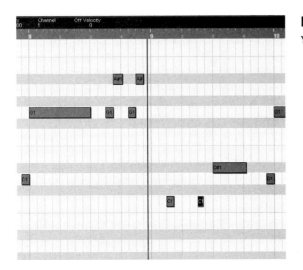

Figure 3.26

Your A#o is now a C1.

Figure 3.27

New settings.

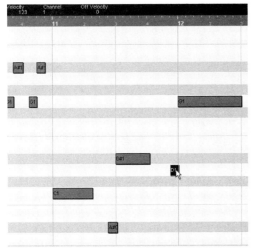

Figure 3.28

The selected D1.

19. Adjust the Length Q to ¼.

20. Click the fifth nudge button once to shorten the note (see Figure 3.30).

43

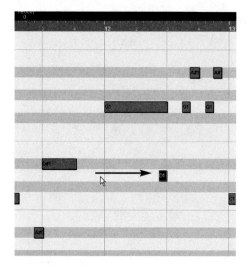

Figure 3.29

The nudged note keeps its relative position.

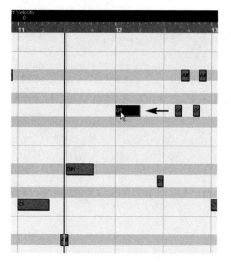

Figure 3.30

The G1 is shortened with a nudge.

21. Change the Quantize value to ¹⁄₁₆.

22. Click the first nudge button once to adjust the note's start time. Once again, compare your progress with what's shown in Figure 3.31.

23. Change the snap type to Events.

24. Using the OST, select the last note of measure 12 (see Figure 3.32).

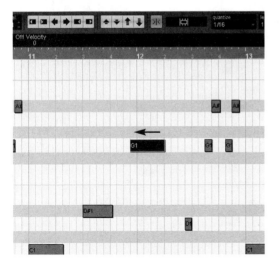

Figure 3.31

The start of the note has been nudged forward.

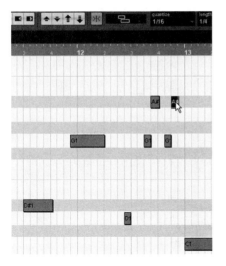

Figure 3.32

Select the note.

25. Using the OST, move the note up against the preceding A#1, noticing how the note "sticks" to the preceding note because of the Events snap type setting (see Figure 3.33).

26. Change the Length Q setting to 1/16.

27. Click the sixth nudge button once to extend the note by a 16th-note increment. Compare your progress with what's shown in Figure 3.34 before moving on.

28. Switch the snap type to Shuffle.

29. Using the OST, select the first A#1 between measures 12 and 13.

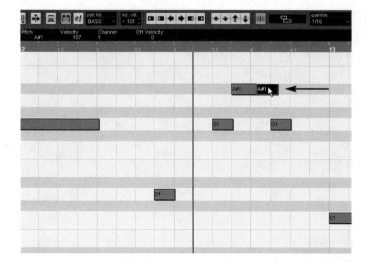

Figure 3.33

The two notes are "stuck together."

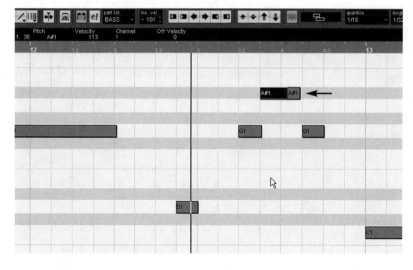

Figure 3.34

A note shortened with a nudge button.

30. Click and drag the note to 4.3 on the ruler. As shown in Figure 3.35, you'll see a green line at point 4.3 on the ruler to indicate that you are at the right location.

31. Release the mouse button. Notice that the A# to the right and the G1 below have swapped places with the original A#. Check your work against what's shown in Figure 3.36 to verify you have followed the steps correctly.

32. Use the forward and rewind buttons on the transport to place your cursor somewhere between measure 12, beat 4.4 on the ruler and measure 13, beat 1 (see Figure 3.37).

33. Change your snap type to Magnetic Cursor.

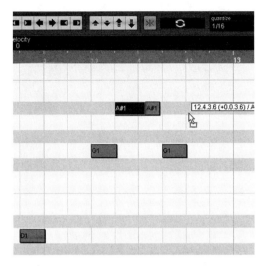

Figure 3.35

The Shuffle green line.

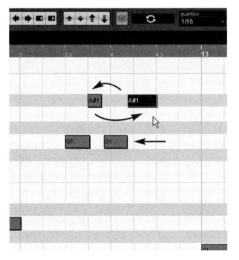

Figure 3.36

The three notes got shuffled around.

34. Change the Quantize setting to 1/1.

35. Using the OST, select the first note at measure 13.

36. Click and drag the note toward the cursor.

37. When the note reaches the cursor, release the mouse button. Notice that because of the Magnetic Cursor snap type setting, the note is moved to the exact position of the cursor. Your result should look something like what appears in Figure 3.38.

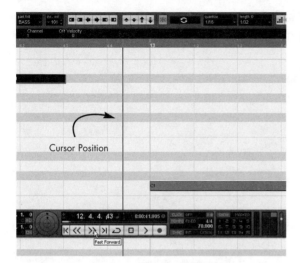

Figure 3.37

Setting up the magnetic cursor.

Figure 3.38

The note sticks to the cursor.

The Step Input and MIDI Edit Buttons

Located to the right of the Length Q display on the toolbar are the Step Input button, marked with six squares in a stair-step pattern, and the MIDI Edit button, which looks like the connector for a MIDI cable (see Figure 3.39). These buttons enable you to create and edit notes in the Key editor. While they are very useful to MIDI programmers, they may at first glance confuse traditional keyboardists, who are used to simply playing and recording their parts the way a pianist would record a piano track. As you'll learn in a moment, both of these buttons use your MIDI keyboard in a not-so-traditional way.

Figure 3.39

The Step Input and Midi Edit buttons.

The Step Input Button

The Step Input tool, although fairly simple, can seem nonsensical to traditional musicians. It uses the MIDI keyboard to create notes in the Note display at a point you designate, but without capturing information about how long or how hard you hit each note. Instead, it uses the setting in the Length Q display to determine the length of each note and the setting in the Quantize display for the placement of sequential notes. You can also adjust the settings so that your MIDI keyboard does not input pitch at all, but still inputs a default note at C3, which can be edited however you like. (If this seems confusing, it won't after you complete the steps in the section "Using the Step Input and MIDI Edit Buttons.")

The MIDI Edit Button

Initially, this button confused me. I thought that because it was next to the Step Input button, it would be a MIDI input button. After a few minutes of frustration, I realized that it was not for keyboard note input in the traditional sense; rather, it was solely for changing the values of MIDI parts that had already been created. Finally, it made sense to me why this button was next to the Step Input button: Although they have completely separate functions, they can be used together to create and alter MIDI notes in yet another useful way. Specifically, when the MIDI Edit button is selected, you can change the selected note's pitch or velocity settings *without* changing the length, start time, or end time—simply by playing it on the MIDI keyboard. After altering the selected note, you can continue altering ensuing notes with each stroke of the keyboard. (Again, if this seems confusing, it won't after you complete the steps in the section "Using the Step Input and MIDI Edit Buttons.")

The Note Buttons

Both the Step Input button and the MIDI Edit button make use of the four buttons located just to their right on the toolbar: the note buttons (see Figure 3.40). These buttons operate as follows:

- **Move Insert Mode button.** The first of the four buttons is the Move Insert Mode button, which is used only with the Step Input button. Activating this button enables you to insert a note within a given area, with the notes to the right moving over to make room. How far these notes to the right move depends on the increment selected in the Quantize display and on how much space is required to accommodate the newly inserted note(s).

Figure 3.40
The note buttons and Mouse Pointer display.

■ **Record Pitch button.** The second note button is the Record Pitch button. When this button is activated, the selected note's pitch is recorded or altered as you play on your MIDI keyboard.

■ **Note On Velocity button.** The third button is the Note On Velocity button. When activated, this button enables you to change the velocity of the selected or newly created note by playing your MIDI keyboard softer or harder.

■ **Note Off Velocity button.** The fourth button, Note Off Velocity, works in the same way as the Note On Velocity button but affects note *off* velocity instead of the more popular note *on* velocity. Again, because using note off velocity is something of a rarity, I won't be demonstrating the Note Off Velocity button in the following exercise. When you're ready to use it, you'll know what to do.

Using the Step Input and MIDI Edit Buttons

This exercise requires the use of your MIDI keyboard controller. By the time you're finished, you may well have turned into the world's fastest sitar player. Remember to use your zoom controllers for easier viewing throughout this exercise.

> **NOTE**
>
> Before you begin this exercise, close the current song and load Song3, found on the CD-ROM that accompanied this book.

1. With Song3 open in the Key editor (you should see a blank screen), click the Step Input button.

2. Click in the Note display at measure 7, beat 1. A blue input line appears, as shown in Figure 3.41. This blue input line shows the point where the new note will be created.

3. Change the Insert Velocity to 20 and the Quantize setting to ¹/₁₆.

> **NOTE**
>
> When using the Step Input button, avoid clicking in the Note display when you *don't* want to change the position of the blue input line—no small task for those people who are a little mouse crazy. To train yourself to avoid this mistake, make it a habit to use the *Mouse Pointer display*, located to the right of the note buttons. The top half of this display is designed to help you guide the mouse to the correct pitch; the bottom half can help you find the exact position of the blue input line.

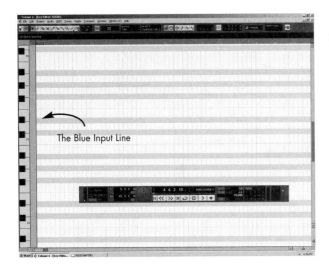

Figure 3.41
Setting up the blue input line.

4. Set the Length Q to Quantize Link. This will make this exercise easier by creating notes that are the same length as the value of your quantize increment setting.

5. With the blue input line on measure 7, beat 1, press any key one time on your MIDI keyboard. After you do, you should see that a note has been created at C3 and on measure 7, beat 1, and that the blue line has moved past the note you just created. Closer examination reveals that the length of the note is $\frac{1}{64}$, and the blue line has moved exactly a $\frac{1}{64}$ note in time. If you were to use the Info Line while selecting the note, you would also see that the note has a velocity of 20. Compare your screen to Figure 3.42 to make sure you're on the right path.

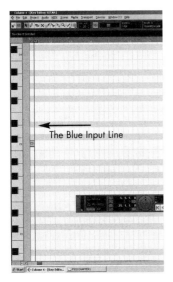

Figure 3.42
A new note is created by using the Step Input tool.

6. Without changing your settings, watch your screen as you continue striking a key on your MIDI keyboard over and over until the blue input line reaches measure 10. Notice that a new note is created at the blue line each time you strike a key, and that the note is always C3 no matter which key you strike on your MIDI keyboard. When you are finished you should have three measures of $^1/_{64}$ notes at C3, as shown in Figure 3.43. (If you do your math or feel like counting, that's 192 C3s between measures 7 and 10.)

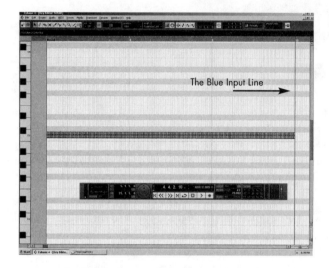

Figure 3.43

The 192 new C3s.

7. Now it's time to work a little harder on your MIDI keyboard. To begin, click the Record Pitch button on the toolbar.

8. With your blue input line at measure 10, beat 1, press the C4 note on your MIDI keyboard. In this case, because the Record Pitch button was activated, you recorded a note at C4 instead of at C3.

9. With your blue input line where you left off in step 8, press D4 on your keyboard, then D#4, then E4, continuing to walk your fingers up the MIDI keyboard until you reach C5. Then walk your fingers back down the keyboard toward B4 until you reach C4.

10. Repeat step 9 one time. You should start to see a visual pattern in the Note display that looks much like the letter M.

11. After reaching the second C4, continue descending down the keyboard until the blue input line reaches measure 11. The last note you hit on the keyboard and created in the Key editor should be an A2. Compare your work to Figure 3.44.

12. Next, go back and insert a piece you forgot. To begin, position the blue input line between the C#3 and C3 just before measure 11.

13. Click the Record Pitch button to de-select it.

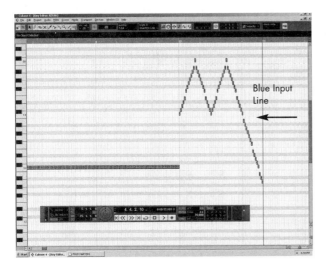

Figure 3.44

Your Step Input masterpiece.

14. Click the Move Insert Mode button to select it.

15. Press any key on the MIDI keyboard three times. Notice that three new notes are created at C3, and that because the Move Insert Mode button was selected, the four notes that were to the right of the C#3 have been moved to the right by the increments designated in the Quantize display. Your new part should look like Figure 3.45.

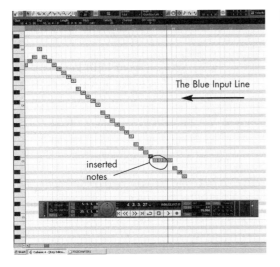

Figure 3.45

The notes you "forgot" have now been inserted.

16. Play back what you've created so far, listening to the world's craziest sitar player. Notice how the first three measures are a little monotonous; let's change them up with the MIDI Edit button.

17. Click the MIDI Edit button. Notice that the blue input line vanishes and the Move Insert Mode button becomes disabled.

18. Using the OST, select the first note you created at measure 7, beat 1.

19. Click the Record Pitch button from among the note buttons.

20. Press C5 once on your MIDI keyboard. The note you selected jumps from C3 to C5 because the MIDI Edit button and the Record Pitch button were selected simultaneously. Also notice that the next note is now selected (see Figure 3.46).

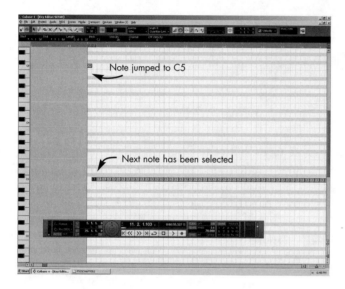

Figure 3.46

Changing the note pitch with the MIDI Edit button.

21. Press B4 on your MIDI keyboard and watch how the following note jumps to B4 in the Note display.

22. Continue walking your fingers down the MIDI keyboard, hitting all black and white keys until you reach C1. Then turn around and walk your fingers back up the keyboard to C5.

23. Repeat step 22 once, but this time stop when you reach B4. When you're finished, compare your work to Figure 3.47.

24. Until now, you've only altered your original note's pitches. You haven't affected the original note's velocity setting of 20 in any way. To do so, first click the Record Pitch button to de-select it.

25. Click the Note On Velocity button to select it.

26. With the OST, select the note (C4) on beat 1 of measure 10.

27. Watching the screen, play any note on the MIDI keyboard very gently. Notice that the following note is selected. That's because you have just recorded a soft velocity setting for the previously selected note.

54

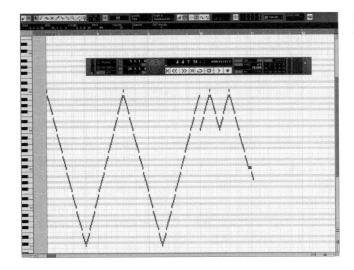

Figure 3.47
Your "MIDI modified" masterpiece!

28. Continue watching the Note display and hitting any key on your MIDI keyboard. This time, however, as you watch the notes get higher in pitch, strike the key *harder.*

29. When the selected note reaches C5, continue striking the key, but hit it more softly each time as the selected note approaches C4.

> **NOTE**
>
> Notice that the key you hit on your MIDI keyboard is used only to send *velocity* information to Cubase. The pitch of the key you strike makes no difference because Cubase uses the pre-recorded pitch from the part you previously created.

30. Unless you examine each note in the Info Line, there is no way to visually check the velocity changes you just made—a tedious task. Instead, check your work by listening to the track, checking to see whether the lower notes seem softer and the higher notes seem harder. If this is the case, you have done your work correctly. Congrats!

The Independent Track Loop Button

Selecting the Independent Track Loop button, which features a ring with an arrow and box on it, enables you to listen to a section of a MIDI part in cycle mode, independently from the rest of the song. You might use the Independent Track Loop button and loop fields display to work on a two-measure section of a bass track while it's repeating, but hear how it sounds as the rest of the track plays in real time. In effect, this feature enables you to *audition* sections of parts under the entire track; its intention is not to stay in loop mode as a part of the song. (There are plenty of ways to loop a part, which I'll discuss later in this book.)

One way to define the start and end times of this independent loop is to use the loop fields display (see Figure 3.48). Another way to adjust the loop start point is to press the Ctrl key on your computer keyboard while clicking the ruler at the spot where you want the loop to start. Alternatively, adjust the loop end point by pressing the Alt key on your computer keyboard while clicking the ruler.

Figure 3.48

The Independent Track Loop button and loop fields display.

> **NOTE**
>
> The Independent Track Loop feature also works in cycle mode. When your song completes its cycle, the independent track loop restarts from the beginning.

When a loop is created, its location is represented in the ruler by the color purple (this color disappears if the Independent Track Loop button is deactivated). You can alter the start and end points of the purple section by simply clicking the loop's start or end point on the ruler with the OST and moving it left or right (see Figure 3.49).

Figure 3.49

The loop's start and end points.

To get a handle on using the Independent Track Loop button—specifically, creating an independent bass loop—do the following:

> **NOTE**
>
> Before you move forward, take a moment to close any songs you may have open in Cubase and load Song1. (For details on how to load Song1, refer to Chapter 1.)

1. With Song1 open, click the Independent Track Loop button to activate it.

2. Change the number in the top loop field display to 7.1.1.0 to start your bass loop at measure 7, beat 1.

3. Change the number in the bottom field display to 9.1.1.0 to end the bass loop at measure 9, beat 1. Notice how the ruler is now purple between measures 7 and 9; this is your independent loop (see Figure 3.50).

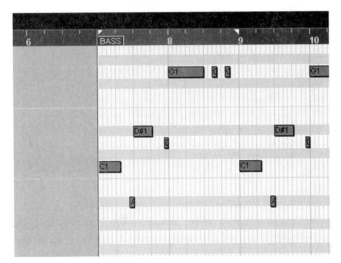

Figure 3.50

Your two-measure independent bass loop.

4. Play the song. As you listen, watch as the same two measures of the bass part loop while the rest of the song continues to play as normal. (To hear this, make sure that the Solo Edit button is *not* activated.)

5. While the track is playing, click the Independent Track Loop button to de-select it. Notice how the purple disappears from the ruler and the track goes back to playing normally.

The Color Scheme Display

The Color Scheme display (see Figure 3.51) color-codes note attributes such as velocity, pitch, MIDI channel, part, or position on the Note display grid (that is, where the note falls between the bars and beats). Unless you're color blind, this can be a helpful tool for maneuvering the Note display. You use the drop-down menu, accessible from the down arrow on the right side of the Color Scheme display, to specify the attribute you want to color-code:

Figure 3.51

The Color Scheme display and menu.

- **Velocity.** When you select this attribute, notes are color-coded according to how hard or softly they are played. Two different colors are used, preferably one light and one dark, with one color fading to the other to represent the dynamic range. (Specify the colors you want to use for your soft and loud velocities by selecting the Setup option in the drop-down list and choosing the colors you'd like to use.)

- **Pitch.** When you select this attribute, notes are displayed using 12 different colors, each representing one of the 12 pitches between C and B on a keyboard. To change the colors used, select the Setup option in the drop-down list and enter the necessary information.

- **Channel.** When you select this attribute, each note is color-coded according to which of the 16 MIDI channels it is set to play back on. To change the colors used, select the Setup option in the drop-down list and enter the necessary information. You probably won't use this setting often; most of the time, all your notes will be set to output on the same MIDI channel. But if you start delving deeper into MIDI, getting really creative, this may come in handy.

- **Part.** When you select this attribute, your part in the Key editor assumes the same color as the color you applied to the part in the project window. This can be useful if you're working with multiple parts, as you will at the end of this chapter. You'll learn how to set part colors in the project window in Chapter 6.

- **GridMatch.** When you select this attribute, you can view each note as a separate color, depending on its relationship to the Note display. That is, the notes positioned at beat 1 at each measure will be one color, the notes positioned at the "and" of beat 1 will be another, and so on with as many as 16 different colors defined. (Note that these colors change as you adjust your Quantize settings for the grid.) This might come in handy if you want to single out all instances of a certain beat from a groove to edit.

The Chord Display

Have you ever come up with a chord on a keyboard that you like the sound of, but you didn't know the name of the chord? If so, you're going to like this little tool. In fact, its only purpose is to indicate what chord (or, if you're not playing a chord, what note) you're playing (see Figure 3.52). To use it, simply position the cursor over a chord you've created; the Chord display will reveal the chord. Be aware, however, that this tool works best with simple chords; it sometimes oversimplifies more complex ones. Instead of relying solely on this tool to reveal chords, think of this feature as a bonus and take a few music-theory lessons so you can more accurately double-check your work.

Figure 3.52
The chord/note display.

The Edit VST Instrument Button

The very last button on the toolbar is the Edit VST Instrument button, which features a mini keyboard and a small arrow (see Figure 3.53). Clicking this button reveals the VST instrument (a virtual synth or sampler plug-in) for the part you are currently working with (unless you're not working with a VST instrument, in which case this button is useless). In addition, it displays the instrument on the screen, enabling you to both access the instrument and change its settings. To try this tool out, click the Edit VST Instrument button with Song1 open. The mono synth appears; either launch the instrument or change its settings as desired.

> **NOTE**
>
> To learn more about the VST instruments included with Cubase 4, explore the manual or check out *Creative Projects with Cubase VST*, published by Thomson Course Technology.

Figure 3.53
The Edit VST Instrument button.

The Controller Lanes and the Line Tool

Chapter 3, "The Toolbar," touched on controllers during its discussion of the Auto Select Controllers button, located on the toolbar. This chapter goes into a lot more detail about how these MIDI controllers function and discusses how they relate to the Key editor. Also, because I skipped over the Line tool earlier, I'll show you how you can use it with a controller lane. Because the Line tool works best with large sections of MIDI events, you'll understand why I waited to discuss this tool in detail until after I discussed the controller lanes. I also touch on using the Line tool within the Note display to create notes.

The Controller Lanes

You can think of a controller as being similar to a slider or knob on, say, a synth. That is, just as you use a slider or knob to control some aspect of the synth, so too do you use controllers to control MIDI. Indeed, every parameter in MIDI can be altered by different types of controllers. For example, various controllers are used to do the following (note that this is only a mere sampling; the list goes on and on):

- Make filter adjustments to synths

- Adjust velocity, pitch, or volume of MIDI notes played back on a synth or sampler

- Change panning from left to right

- Start and stop your song in Cubase

- Change the program settings on your synth

- Control a group of controllers

Although there are more than 120 available MIDI controllers, most people use fewer than 10 at a time. You can delve more deeply into the controllers, but the deeper you go, the more technical it becomes. If you want to go there, you'll need to know how to speak in hex and binary. To keep things simple, this book discusses what I consider to be the top five basic Cubase controllers: velocity, pitch bend, volume, pan, and modulation.

A *controller lane* is similar to the Note display, except instead of showing notes, it displays *controller events* (which are essentially data used to define a controller's setting). Each type of controller, be it velocity, pitch, or what have you, has its own controller lane. The primary purpose of a controller lane is to enable you to edit a controller; you modify the controller events in a controller lane with the same tools you use to modify notes in the Note display.

Let's take a moment to explore controller lanes. First, close any songs you may have open in Cubase and launch Song4 from the CD-ROM that accompanies this book. The song opens in the Key editor. Unlike the previous demos, this song contains two controller lanes, just below the Note display: the top one for the velocity controller and the bottom one for the pitch bend (see Figure 4.1 and Figure 4.2).

Figure 4.1

Controller lanes in the Key editor.

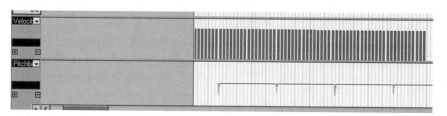

Figure 4.2

The velocity and pitch bend controller lanes up close.

Notice how the events that have been recorded in each lane are displayed differently. The velocity lane shows an event, represented by a vertical bar, for each note in the Note display above. The top of the vertical bar shows the velocity level of the corresponding note; the higher the bar, the harder the note is played, and vice versa. In contrast, the events in the pitch bend controller lane, which look more like sound waves than vertical bars, appear as something completely unrelated to the position of the notes on the grid. That's because the pitch bend was created using the pitch bend wheel of a MIDI keyboard at different locations throughout the part rather than on each individual note.

Regardless of what type of controller they manage, controller lanes have a few other features. If you look closely at the left side of each lane, you will notice an abbreviated form of the words "velocity" (see Figure 4.3) and "pitch bend." To edit a different type of controller, click the down arrow next to the controller lane's name and choose the controller type from the drop-down list that appears. Note that this area of the controller lane also features a Mouse Pointer display, which reflects the mouse's current position in relation to the parameter of its related controller lane. Below the Mouse Pointer display are two small boxes, one with a plus (+) sign and one with a minus (–) sign; you'll learn more about these in a moment.

Figure 4.3
Controller lane setup.

Adjusting the Height of the Controller Lane

In addition to using the zoom controls to adjust your view, you can make the lane shorter or taller to reduce or expand your view. For example, you might expand the lane such that it stretches over the Note display to provide a better view for precision work, and then contract it when you're finished. To do so, position your OST on the top line of the controller lane; a double-sided arrow appears. When it does, simply click and drag the line up or down (see Figure 4.4) to expand or contract the lane.

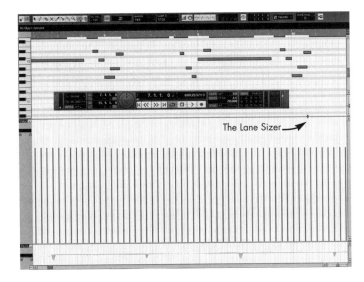

Figure 4.4
Sizing the lanes.

Hiding a Controller Lane

You've worked on parts in the Key editor that didn't show controller lanes. That's not to say, however, that there weren't any events recorded. Rather, the controller lanes were simply hidden. Controller lanes simply contain visual representations of controller events. They do not contain the controller events themselves. Regardless of whether the controller lane is visible, the controller events in the song still exist.

To hide a controller lane, do the following:

1. Click the Solo Edit button to enable it. That way, you'll hear the guitar track only.

2. Click Play on the transport. You should hear only the guitar part playing. (Because this song was set up in Cycle mode, it will loop until you click Stop on the transport.)

3. As the track plays, click the minus (–) button in the pitch bend controller lane. The pitch bend controller lane vanishes, but the track still plays as normal. That's because you haven't changed the *controller events* in any way; you merely hid the controller lane.

4. As the track continues to play, right-click anywhere in the velocity controller lane and choose Remove This Lane from the pop-up menu that appears. The velocity lane disappears. Just as when you clicked the minus (–) button, the sound of the track you are listening to is not affected.

5. Click Stop on the transport before you give yourself a headache listening to the guitar part over and over.

Adding Controller Lanes and Selecting MIDI Controllers

If you've hidden a controller lane but you now want to reveal it, don't worry. I can show you how to bring them back. I'll also show you how to add more controller lanes from the list of over 120 available MIDI controllers.

1. Using the OST, right-click anywhere within the Note display and choose Create a New Controller Lane in the pop-up menu that appears. A velocity controller lane is created.

> **NOTE**
>
> Anytime you create a new controller lane, it's a velocity controller lane by default, regardless of whether you already have a velocity controller lane set up.

2. Using the OST, click the plus (+) box in the velocity controller lane to create a new velocity controller lane.

3. Repeat step 2; you now have three velocity controller lanes.

4. Open the drop-down list in the second velocity controller lane and choose Pitch Bend. The controller lane changes from a velocity controller lane to a pitch bend controller lane.

5. Open the drop-down menu in the bottom velocity controller lane and select Pan. The controller lane changes from a velocity controller lane to a pan controller lane.

As you can see, changing the controllers displayed is as easy as selecting them from a drop-down list. See a close-up of the three new controller lanes in Figure 4.5.

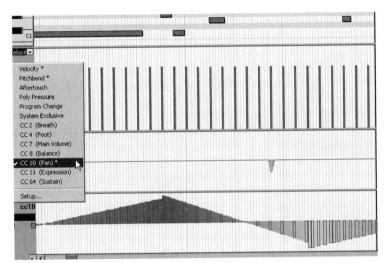

Figure 4.5
The new controller lanes and drop-down list.

NOTE

If you don't see the controller type you need in the drop-down list, choose Setup and select the desired controller from the list on the right. Also, because you probably won't use all 120+ controllers, you can click the Setup option in the drop-down list and specify which controllers you want available from the drop-down menu.

Another Look at the Auto Select Controllers Button

The Auto Select Controllers button enables you to automatically select a controller's events that occur at the same place on the grid that a selected note occurs. Here's how it works:

1. With the OST, click the note at measure 7, beat 1. (Make sure that the Auto Select Controllers button is not yet activated.) Notice that there is nothing selected in the pitch or pan controller lanes.

> **NOTE**
>
> In this exercise, the velocity is selected in the velocity lane because the velocity is a part of the note by default. The pitch and pan controllers act completely independently of the notes, which is why they are *not* selected when you select a note without enabling the Auto Select Controllers button.

2. Using the Erase tool, erase the note at measure 7, beat 1. Notice that nothing changes in the pan and pitch bend controller lanes.

3. Click the Auto Select Controllers button on the toolbar to activate it.

4. Using the OST, click the note at measure 9, beat 1. Notice how the events in the pitch bend and pan controller lanes are also selected for the duration of the note you clicked (see Figure 4.6).

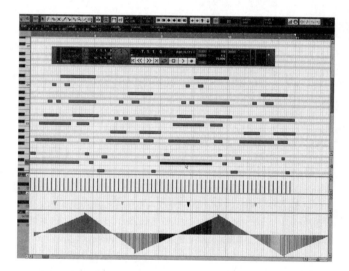

Figure 4.6

The controller lanes are selected.

5. Using the Erase tool, erase the selected note at measure 9. Notice how the events in the controller lanes change; the settings that occurred during the duration of the note have vanished, canceling the controller events that occurred between the start and end points of the deleted note. (Notice how the last controller event before the deleted note remains in place, creating a "flat line" until the next controller event occurs just past where the recently deleted controller events ended.) This can be a useful editing feature when you have deliberately linked your controller lane events to notes in the Note display (see Figure 4.7).

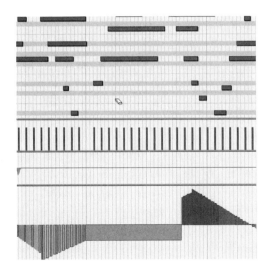

Figure 4.7
The events you had created in the controller lanes have vanished with the erased note.

Editing in a Controller Lane

As mentioned earlier, you can use most of the tools described so far for editing notes in a controller lane. Since those tools have been covered already, I won't cover them again here; instead, I urge you to experiment with using these various tools (particularly the tool buttons) in each of the controller lanes.

Using the Line Tool

The Line tool is one of the most useful tools for making dramatic changes in a controller lane. That's because controller lanes often contain many events, and the Line tool works best when simultaneously editing a large number of events. The Line tool uses various line patterns to draw the values of several events at once as opposed to entering a value for each individual event.

Editing with the Line Tool in a Controller Lane

If you click the down arrow in the bottom-right corner of the Line button, you'll see a drop-down list containing several different types of "lines" that you can use when editing: line, parabola, sine, triangle, square, and paint. To get a handle on how each one works, follow these steps:

1. Click the down arrow in the bottom-right corner of the Line button and choose Line from the drop-down list that appears.

2. Position the crosshair pointer at measure 7, beat 1 in the velocity controller lane, toward the bottom of the first vertical bar. The velocity lane's Mouse Pointer display should read 0.

67

3. Click and drag the mouse upward and to the right so that the crosshair pointer is at measure 8, beat 1 and the Mouse Pointer display reads 127. A diagonal line path is created from your start point to your current location (see Figure 4.8).

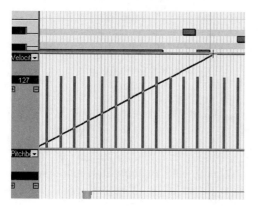

Figure 4.8

The Line tool and line path.

4. Release the mouse button. Notice that your vertical velocity bars have been adjusted to match the path you created using the Line tool, forming an ascending velocity pattern between measures 7 and measure 8 (see Figure 4.9).

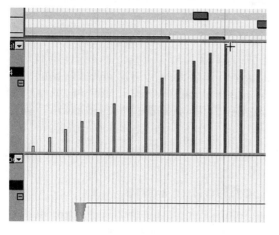

Figure 4.9

Newly sized velocity bars.

5. Play back the track. Notice how the notes sound as if they are played harder (and, in this case, louder) as they move from measure 7 to measure 8.

6. Using the Line tool again, create a descending slope from measure 8, beat 1 to measure 9, beat 1, starting at 127 in the Mouse Pointer display and going to 0. When you're finished, it should look like what's shown in Figure 4.10.

7. Repeat the pattern you created between measures 7 and 9 between measures 9 and 11, as shown in Figure 4.11.

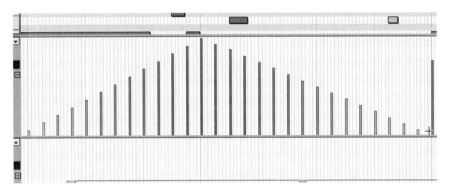

Figure 4.10

Up and down with velocity.

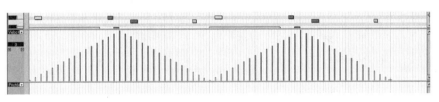

Figure 4.11

Virtual "mountains" of velocity.

8. Play back the track and listen to what you've accomplished. Congratulations! You have created what musicians refer to as *dynamics* in the guitar part.

9. Repeat steps 1–8, but this time change your Line tool to a parabola by choosing Parabola in the Line tool's drop-down list. When you're finished, your velocity controller lane should look like a pair of shark fins (see Figure 4.12).

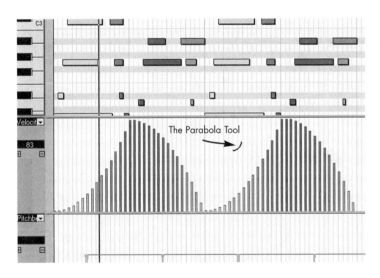

Figure 4.12

Parabola "fins."

10. Play back the track, noticing the subtle difference in the velocity pattern. The ascent has a little sharper curve to it, and the descent has a slightly softer curve.

11. Choose Square in the Line tool's drop-down list.

12. Change your Quantize setting to 1/8.

13. Place the square Line tool on the pan controller lane at measure 7, beat 1 so that it rests on the lane's middle dividing line, at point 0 in the Mouse Pointer display.

14. Click and drag the mouse downward and to the right to measure 11, beat 1; the Mouse Pointer display should read −64 when the pointer is at measure 11 (see Figure 4.13).

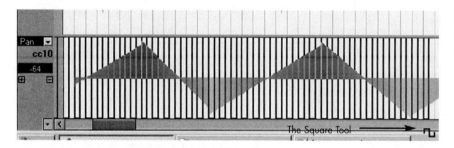

Figure 4.13

Using the square Line tool.

15. Release the mouse button. Your pan controller lane should look something like the example shown in Figure 4.14.

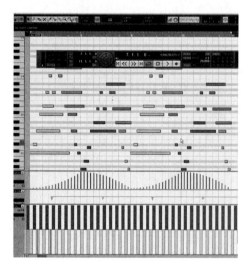

Figure 4.14

Panning "squares."

16. Play back the track, listening to the crazy panning effect you just created. Every other note jumps from left to right in your monitors as the track plays. The sound is either right or left because the square Line tool is cold and abrupt, and is therefore harsh in its divisions.

17. Select Sine from the Line tool's drop-down list and repeat steps 13–16, this time using the sine Line tool. When you're finished, instead of having a block pattern, you have a wave type pattern, as shown in Figure 4.15.

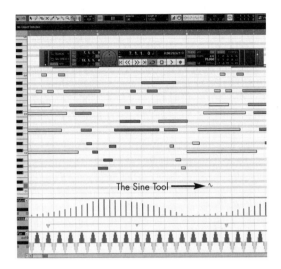

Figure 4.15

The panning sine wave.

The Sine Tool ⟶ ᶺ

18. Play back the track. Notice that the guitar is still panning back and forth between the speakers. This time, however, instead of jumping hard left and hard right, the notes have a smoother pan between the left and right stereo fields.

NOTE

The Quantize setting in the Quantize display determines how long a waveform will be when using the sine, triangle, or square tool from the Line tool's drop-down list.

19. Prepare to get seasick! Select Triangle from the Line tool's drop-down list.

20. Change the Quantize setting to 1/1 in the Quantize display.

21. Position the triangle Line tool at measure 7, beat 1 on the middle dividing line of the pitch bend controller lane dividing line, at point 0 in the Mouse Pointer display.

22. Click and drag the mouse pointer downward and to the right just before measure 9 so that the Mouse Pointer display reads –8192 (see Figure 4.16).

23. Starting at measure 9, beat 1, click and drag the mouse pointer upward and to the right so that the number 8191 is displayed in the Mouse Pointer display.

24. Release the mouse button just before measure 11. Your pitch bend controller lane should appear similar to the example shown in Figure 4.17.

25. Play the track back from the transport and try to hold down your lunch as you listen. This is what happens when you go overboard with the pitch bend controller!

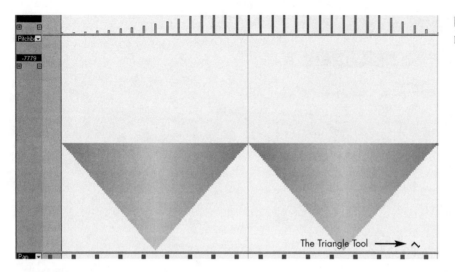

Figure 4.16
Downward triangles.

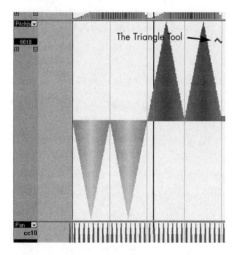

Figure 4.17
Downward and upward triangles.

> **NOTE**
>
> The pitch bend controller works within the limits set on the instrument's pitch bend range. In this exercise, the pitch bend has a subtle bending effect because the synth's range is set to one whole step. A lot of synths allow you to adjust the pitch bend range up to two octaves, which would create a much more dramatic effect.

Clicking and dragging the paint Line tool in a manner similar to that used with the other Line tools enables you to create your own freehand patterns, making it great for helping you get the exact edit you're looking for. For example, in Figure 4.18, see how I destroyed all the pretty work you just did using the paint Line tool and my art skills?

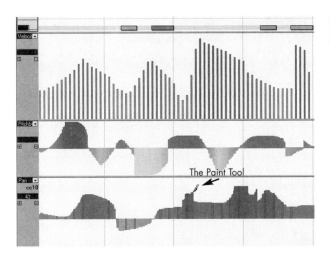

Figure 4.18

My controller lane work of art.

Creating Notes in the Note Display Using the Line Tool

Even though I think the Line tool works best as an editor in the controller lanes, it can also be used to create notes in the Note display. Here's how:

1. Close the current song and load Song3, found on the CD-ROM that accompanies this book.

2. Click the Line button.

3. Change the Quantize setting in the Quantize display to 1/64.

4. Change the Length Q to Quantize Link.

5. Set the Insert Velocity to 20.

> **NOTE**
>
> Before using the Line tool to create notes in the Note display, you must tell Cubase what velocity you would like the notes to have and how long you would like each note to be. To do so, enter your settings into the Insert Velocity, Quantize, and Length Q fields before you create any note with the Line tool. Otherwise, the notes you create will use the currently displayed settings by default.

6. Zoom in on the Key editor's Note display for a close-up view of measure 7 to measure 8 only.

7. Click the Solo Editor button.

8. With the Line tool, click and drag the mouse upward and to the right from the start of measure 7, beat 1 to the start of measure 8, beat 1, starting at C4 and ending at C7.

9. When you reach C7 at measure 8, release the mouse button. The Line tool creates an ascending pattern of notes from measure 7 to measure 8, as shown in Figure 4.19.

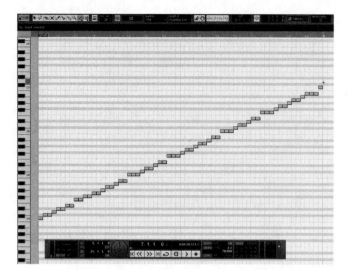

Figure 4.19
A line of notes has been created.

Play back the track to hear your creation and, if you'd like, try using the other options in the Line tool's drop-down list to create notes. You will find that the line, parabola, and paint options work best; the other options usually just create a horizontal pattern of the same starting note.

5 The MIDI Menu

I consider the MIDI menu the gateway to the world of MIDI editing because it essentially acts as the front door to everything MIDI in Cubase. Whether you are working in the project window, the Key editor, or any other editor, the MIDI menu—which, along with 10 other menu options, is located on the menu bar at the top of every Cubase screen (see Figure 5.1)—can take you wherever you need to go in Cubase's MIDI kingdom. To access the menu, simply click the word MIDI (see Figure 5.2).

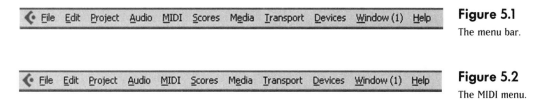

Figure 5.1
The menu bar.

Figure 5.2
The MIDI menu.

The Gateway to the MIDI Editors

So far, you've done a lot of MIDI editing in the Key editor (and you are about to do a lot more). But because you've been working with demo songs that I created, you've entered the Key editor through the back door, opening songs that were saved with the Key editor window active in the display. To enter the Key editor through the front door, as it were, you use the MIDI menu. To do so, open the MIDI menu and choose Open Key Editor (see Figure 5.3). Regardless of what you're working on, Cubase will launch the Key editor, with the part of your song that is currently selected displayed.

> **NOTE**
>
> In addition to opening the Key editor from the MIDI menu, you can also launch Cubase's four other editors: the Score editor, the Drum editor, the List editor, and the In- Place editor. You'll work with all these editors later in the book.

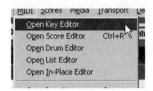

Figure 5.3

The MIDI menu's editor options.

Quantize Options

Just below the MIDI menu's editor options are three quantize options with which you should concern yourself now: Over Quantize, Iterative Quantize, and Advanced Quantize (see Figure 5.4). If you found my earlier discussion of quantization a little confusing, seeing these options may make you panic. The good news is that these options aren't as mystifying as they seem; the better news is that I'm skipping over them for now. You'll explore these options in Chapter 8, "A Closer Look at Quantizing MIDI."

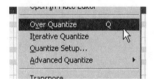

Figure 5.4

The Quantize options.

The Transpose Function

To *transpose* a note is to change its pitch. So far, you've experimented with changing pitches using the OST, the Info Line, the nudge buttons, and the MIDI editing button. These methods work well when you only want to change one or two notes, but what if you want to change several notes in a part at once, and you want to be picky about pitch changes? That's where Cubase's Transpose function, located below the MIDI menu's quantize options, comes in. To use it, use the OST to select the range of notes you want to transpose, open the MIDI menu, and choose Transpose; Cubase launches the Transpose dialog box, shown in Figure 5.5.

As you can see, this dialog box is set up to enable you to make some quick and simple changes. For example, to alter the pitch of the selected notes, adjust the Semitones setting up or down. This setting works in half steps; that means, for example, that if you want to move the pitch of the selected notes two whole steps down on the scale, you would enter −4, the − meaning "down" and the 4 meaning four half steps, or two whole steps. (Some knowledge of music theory could really help you choose the "right" pitch change for your selected notes, but you can always just

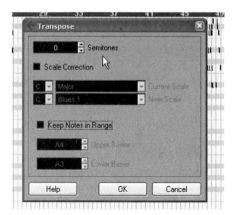

Figure 5.5
The Transpose function.

play around with it, using your ear to decide.) In addition, you can change the scale used, which essentially tells Cubase how to quantize your pitch when the Transpose function is used.

Let's take a moment to explore the Transpose function. First, close any songs you may have open in Cubase and launch Song6 from the CD-ROM that accompanied this book. Then do the following:

1. With Song6 open, use the OST to select the ascending C Major scale between measures 2 and 3.

2. Open the MIDI menu and choose Transpose.

3. Make sure the Semitones setting is set to 0.

4. Click the Scale Correction checkbox to check it.

5. Open the Current Scale drop-down list and choose C Major.

6. Open the New Scale drop-down list and choose C Blues 1.

> **NOTE**
>
> When using the drop-down menu, you can see there are quite a few different scale types to choose from.

7. Click OK. The third and seventh notes in the C Major scale change to create the C Blues scale. To double-check your work, compare it to the finished example between measures 30 and 31.

Being able to quantize your pitches according to scale means you don't have to be a music-theory wizard to get your scales right. Cubase knows the scales, so it can do the work for you. If you change the key center of a scale, Cubase will alter the notes accordingly but keep the notes as close as possible to their current position on the scale.

> **NOTE**
>
> The scale that most musicians are probably familiar with is the *chromatic* scale, which simply moves from C to C on a piano keyboard, hitting every white and black key in between. Cubase refers to this scale as "no scale" because just moving up and down on a keyboard really doesn't give you a pitch center.

The other great feature of the Transpose function is that it enables you to set high and low limits on your pitch quantize. Because every instrument has its own physical range limitations, this feature can come in handy if you want to achieve some realistic-sounding parts. For example, if you were recording a bass guitar part, you might set your low-limit pitch to a low E to prevent you from creating a part that a normal bass player wouldn't be able to play. To get a handle on this feature, follow these steps, which will limit the range of a two-octave part to one octave:

1. With Song6 open, use the OST to select the notes between measures 3 and 5.

2. Launch the MIDI menu and choose Transpose.

3. Make sure the Semitones setting is at 0.

4. Uncheck the Scale Correction checkbox.

5. Click the Keep Notes in Range checkbox to check it.

6. Change the Upper Barrier setting to A4.

7. Change the Lower Barrier setting to A3.

8. Click OK. The pitches that went from C2 to C4 have been altered so that only notes between A3 and A4 are played. Notice that the notes have not been deleted, merely moved so that they are played within the range settings. To double-check your work, compare it to the finished example between measures 31 and 33.

The MIDI Functions Menu

Below the Transpose entry in the MIDI menu are several functions: Merge MIDI in Loop, Freeze MIDI Modifiers, Dissolve Part, O-Note Conversion, and Repeat Loop. These features are disabled because they cannot be used within the Key editor; you'll learn about them later, when you explore Cubase's other editors.

What I'd like to go over now are some very useful editing tools that can be employed in several editors, including the Key editor. These tools are accessible from the MIDI menu's Functions submenu, also called the *MIDI Functions menu* (see Figure 5.6). This menu contains access to 16 MIDI functions, discussed in the next several sections.

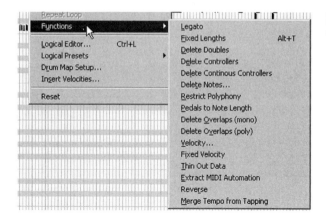

Figure 5.6
The MIDI Functions menu.

Legato

The first of these MIDI functions is the Legato function. Those of you who are familiar with this term know that it means "played smoothly" or "tied together." As such, you can use the Legato function to extend the length of every note such that they are held together, with the end time of one note touching the start time of the note that follows.

Here's how to use the Legato function:

1. With Song6 open, use the OST to select the first three notes of measure 6, noticing how they are played short, or *staccato*.

2. Open the MIDI menu, choose Functions, and select Legato. Notice how the selected notes are now held together.

3. Play back the track so you can hear the difference, comparing your work to the first three notes in measure 34.

Fixed Lengths

This handy function makes it possible for you to alter the lengths of several notes simultaneously such that they are all the same. This is very useful for tightening a part created using a MIDI keyboard or instrument. After all, even if the notes were written to be all of the same length, the notes, when performed by a human, will most likely vary slightly in length. To correct the lengths with this function, change your Length Q setting to the desired note length, as shown here:

1. With Song6 open, use the OST to select the last three notes between measures 6 and 7. Notice how each note has a different length.

2. Change your Length Q setting to 1/16.

3. Open the MIDI menu, choose Functions, and select Fixed Lengths. The three notes are converted to 1/16 notes.

4. Play back the track so you can hear the difference, comparing your work to the last three notes between measures 34 and 35.

Delete Doubles

A doubled note is usually not something you want when you're creating a MIDI part. Doubled notes often happen during quantization, when one note is pulled to the same exact place as another note on the grid. They can also occur when you overdub a part and play over an existing note.

Just how a doubled note sounds usually depends on the sound you are using with your synth or sampler. Sometimes, the effect of a doubled note is not noticeable. Other times, however, the doubled note creates a phased sound. Although you might sometimes like this effect, it is often unwanted.

One way to eliminate a doubled note is to delete either one of the notes by clicking it with the Erase tool. This works well if you're dealing with relatively few doubled notes. If, however, your part contains multiple doubled notes, using the Erase tool to eliminate them can get a little monotonous. Fortunately, Cubase includes the Delete Doubles function, which offers the best way to delete multiple nuisance doubled notes. Here's how it works:

1. First, create a part with some doubled notes. To begin, with Song 6 open, use the OST to select the last two beats of 1/16 notes between measure 7, beat 3 and measure 8, beat 1.

2. Move the eight selected notes, placing them directly above the first eight notes in measure 7. Although it appears as if there are only eight notes at the start of measure 7, there are in fact eight *doubled* notes.

3. Using the OST, select the first eight doubled notes in measure 7.

4. Open the MIDI menu, choose Functions, and select Delete Doubles.

5. To verify that the doubled notes have been eliminated, use the OST to select the first note at measure 7, beat 1 and move it to measure 7, beat 3. When you do, you will see that there was no note under the note you just moved; that's because you deleted the doubled notes. To check your work, compare it to the finished example between measures 35 and 36.

Delete Controllers and Delete Continuous Controllers

So far, I've discussed MIDI controllers and controller lanes. Now, possibly for the first time, you've run into the phrase "continuous controllers." A *continuous controller* is a type of controller; indeed, a continuous controller has the same features as a controller, except it contains two extra bytes of data, meaning it allows for more detailed, finer increments. A pitch bend wheel is an example of a continuous controller because instead of limiting your ability to change your pitch in increments between 0 and 127 only, it can change in increments from 0 to in the thousands.

The bummer with Cubase is that it doesn't really tell you whether a particular controller is a continuous controller or a regular controller; you're just expected to know. Here's a good rule of thumb: If the device used to control the controller (such as a pitch bend wheel, mod wheel, knob, slider, or button) works in an on/off fashion, it's probably *not* a continuous controller. If, on the other hand, the device operates the way a gas pedal functions on a car, with a high and a low setting and a bunch of vague settings in between, it is most likely a continuous controller.

As you probably guessed, the Delete Controllers and Delete Continuous Controllers functions enable you to eliminate controller and continuous controller events, respectively. These functions prevent you from having to select events in a controller lane and use the Erase tool to delete them. In fact, using this feature, you don't even need to have a controller lane open to eliminate controller events.

> **NOTE**
>
> The key point here is that when you select Delete Controllers, *all* controller events (including continuous controller events) in the selected part—*not* just the selected events within the part—are erased. If you want to get rid of just the continuous controller events, use the Delete Continuous Controllers function.

These MIDI functions can come in handy, especially when you're working with a large a part that you would like to wipe clean of controller events.

Delete Notes

The next option in the MIDI Functions menu, Delete Notes, appears to be pretty simple, but in fact offers several options (see Figure 5.7). Instead of just enabling you to erase an unwanted note or group of notes, you can use this function to set up more specific guidelines with regard to which notes get erased, perhaps using the length and/or the velocity of each selected note as parameters. One scenario in which this could be very useful is for getting rid of what some people call "ghost notes" in a performance. (*Ghost notes* are notes that usually occur when a performer's hand rests on a key or two or when a drummer's stick bumps the drum head during a performance). To see this function's potential, do the following:

1. Using the OST, select the group of notes between measures 8 and 10.
2. Open the MIDI menu, choose Functions, and select Delete Notes.
3. Click the Minimum Length checkbox to select it.
4. Type 144 in the Minimum Length field.
5. Click the Minimum Velocity checkbox to select it.

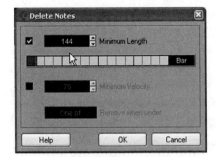

Figure 5.7

The Delete Notes dialog box.

6. Type 75 in the Minimum Velocity field.

7. Open the Remove When Under list and choose One Of (which means *either* the length or the velocity).

8. Click OK. Every note that had either a velocity below 75 or a length shorter than 144 is deleted. This should leave you with two notes; check your work against the completed example between measures 36 and 38.

Restrict Polyphony

Although the next function in the list, Restrict Polyphony, sounds pretty fancy, it's really just another way to delete notes you don't want. Specifically, this function erases the notes in a chord, starting from the bottom of the chord pitch-wise and working its way up to the top so you don't lose your *top note voicing*, which, in most cases, contains an important melodic element and is often the most audible part of the chord.

> **NOTE**
>
> *Polyphony* means "many voices," which in most musical cases means "more than one pitch at a time." A polyphonic synthesizer can play several notes, or "voices," at once, whereas a monophonic synthesizer or instrument can play only one note at a time.

You may be wondering why you would want to *restrict* an instrument from playing a chord. The answer could be that you are trying to emulate the performance of a particular real instrument that is naturally restricted from playing more than one or two notes at time (such as a flute or a saxophone). Alternatively, maybe you just want to lessen the load on your polyphonic synthesizer or thin out an arrangement that sounds too muddy. Whatever your reasons for restricting polyphony, this is the tool. Here's how it works:

1. Using the OST, select the notes between measures 14 and 16.

2. Open the MIDI menu, choose Functions, and select Restrict Polyphony. A dialog box (shown in Figure 5.8) opens.

Figure 5.8

The Allow dialog box, for restricting polyphony.

3. Restrict the polyphony to two voices by changing the Voices setting to 2.

4. Click OK. The triads (three-note chords) that appeared between measures 14 and 16 should now just be two-note chords. Compare your work with the finished example between measures 42 and 44.

Pedals to Note Length

Sometimes, a performer removes his hands from the keys while keeping his foot on the sustain pedal. Although there's nothing wrong with this practice, the note as it appears in the MIDI recording may appear shorter than it needs to. In my view, the primary purpose of this function is to capture the sustained note in printed score form, or if you want to remove the controller but keep the notes held longer.

This is because a note sustained by using a controller usually sounds a little different from a note that is held, and using this function will usually alter the sound of the part. Sometimes this is okay, but other times the end result of this type of edit can create a sound that you're not looking for. The function works by looking for on/off events in the sustain controller and changing the notes' lengths to match the controller's off events. If the performer had a heavy foot—that is, if he didn't release the sustain pedal until the end—only the last note's length will be changed because the off event doesn't occur until after the last note.

Delete Overlaps (Mono and Poly)

An *overlap* is when a note plays over the note that follows. This sometimes creates an undesirable effect, especially when using a mono instrument. In most cases, this is caused by human error; for example, a keyboardist might let a finger rest on a key a little too long, playing the next note in a piece of music before finishing the one before.

You can rectify this by using the Delete Overlaps function. If the notes that overlap are of the same pitch, use the Mono version of the tool; if the notes that overlap are of different pitches, then the Poly version applies. Here's an example of deleting an overlap:

1. Select the notes from measure 16, beat 3 to measure 19. Notice how some notes overlap others (see Figure 5.9).

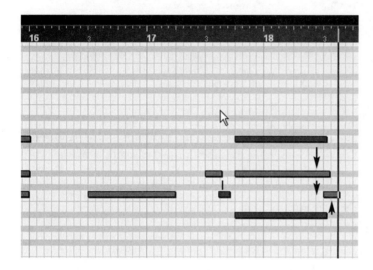

Figure 5.9
Overlapping notes.

2. Open the MIDI menu, choose Functions, and select Delete Overlaps (Mono). Notice how the end of the note that was originally overlapping has been adjusted to fix the problem (see Figure 5.10). Check your work against measures 44 through 47.

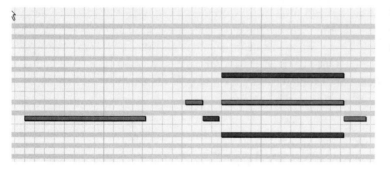

Figure 5.10
The lengths of the overlapping notes have been adjusted.

Velocity and Fixed Velocity

I know, you've already explored at least half a dozen ways to change velocity settings, but here are two more:

- **Velocity.** You use the Velocity function when you have a group of notes that all have different velocities, and you want to change the overall velocity for the entire group of notes with or without affecting how the individual note velocities relate to the other notes in the group.

- **Fixed Velocity.** You use the Fixed Velocity function to change the velocities of the selected notes to one uniform setting. This is very similar to the way you create a note using the Insert Velocity display on the toolbar.

Choosing Velocity from the MIDI Function menu opens the Velocity dialog box (see Figure 5.11). It offers three options for editing velocity. The first is a simple add/subtract method, which raises or lowers the velocity of the entire selected group by the number you specify. The second option compresses or expands the dynamic range according to a ratio setting you enter (this is similar to how an audio compressor works with an audio signal). The third option is a limiting method, which acts much like an audio limiter by creating a ceiling and a floor, which velocities cannot go over and under, respectively. Because these methods are quite different, I demonstrate all of them in the upcoming exercise.

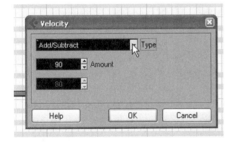

Figure 5.11

The Velocity dialog box.

The Fixed Velocity function works similarly to the Insert Velocity display on the toolbar, except that it works with notes that have already been created. To get a handle on using both the Velocity and Fixed Velocity functions, follow these steps:

1. Using the OST, select the notes between measures 65 and 67.

2. Open the MIDI menu, choose Functions, and select Velocity. The Velocity dialog box opens; notice in the controller lane under the dialog box how the velocities of the selected notes range from fairly high to fairly low.

3. Open the Type drop-down list and choose Add/Subtract.

4. Change the value in the Amount field to −20.

5. Click OK. Notice how the velocity decreases by 20 on each selected note, but the difference in velocity between each selected note remains the same. Check your work against measures 68 through 70.

6. Using the OST, select the notes between measures 71 and 73.

7. Once again, open the MIDI menu, choose Functions, and select Velocity. The Velocity dialog box opens.

8. Open the Type drop-down list and select Compress/Expand.

9. Set the ratio at 50 percent.

10. Click OK. Notice how the lower velocities have been raised, but the higher velocities are largely unaffected. Compare your work to measures 74 through 76.

11. Using the OST, select the notes between measures 77 and 79.

12. Once again, open the MIDI menu, choose Functions, and select Velocity. The Velocity dialog box opens.

13. Open the Type drop-down list and choose Limit.

14. Set the upper limit to 90.

15. Set the lower limit to 80.

16. Click OK. Notice how the lower velocities have risen to the low setting of 80, and the higher velocities have been lowered to the high setting of 90, while velocities in between have not been affected. Compare your work to measures 80 through 82.

17. Using the OST, select the notes between measures 82 and 85.

18. Set the Insert Velocity to 120 on the toolbar.

19. Open the MIDI menu, choose Functions, and select Fixed Velocity. Notice how every selected velocity has been changed to 120. Compare your work to measures 86 through 88.

20. If you haven't listened to the dynamic changes you've made throughout this exercise, listen to measures 65 through 88 so you can hear what's happening with each type of velocity edit.

Thin Out Data

The main purpose of the next MIDI function, Thin Out Data, is to reduce the load on your synths and samplers. This function was designed specifically for use with continuous controllers, where a lot of data in fine increments has been recorded. Basically, the function tries to give you something that sounds pretty close to the original recording that used the continuous controller settings, but in larger increments, so that it doesn't overheat your synth's CPU (and if you're using a virtual synth, I'm talking about your computer). To use the Thin Out Data function, you simply need to select the part you want to thin out and then choose Thin Out Data from the MIDI Functions menu.

> **NOTE**
>
> Using the Thin Out Data function may change the graphical appearance of the controller events in the controller lanes, but not in a dramatic way.

Extract MIDI Automation

To *extract* MIDI automation is to convert your controller information into automation tracks, which can be viewed and edited just like any other automation track in the project window. After the controllers have been converted into automation tracks, the continuous controllers and controller lanes are deleted from your MIDI part.

> **NOTE**
>
> In the earliest version of Cubase 4, the controller lanes and controller events remained intact after MIDI automation was extracted. This bug has been fixed in the latest version, 4.0.2. If you haven't downloaded the latest update to Cubase 4, I highly recommend you visit Steinberg's web site at http://www.steinberg.net, where you can download the most recent update.

Reverse

The Reverse function enables you to switch the notes around so that they play from end to start as opposed to start to end. Unlike reversing audio, this actually reverses the notes, not the recording, resulting in a much different effect. Here's how it works:

1. Using the OST, select the range of notes between measures 20 and 22.

2. Play the part back so you get a good idea of how it sounds.

3. Open the MIDI menu, choose Functions, and select Reverse. The note that originally ended the short piece now starts the measures, and the note that originally started the measures is now at the end.

4. Play back the track so you can hear the difference. You can compare your work to the completed exercise between measures 48 and 50.

Merge Tempo from Tapping

The last of the 16 MIDI functions, Merge Tempo from Tapping, works similarly to the Time Warp tool in that it works primarily with the tempo track. It enables you to tap along with a recording; as you tap, a MIDI track is created, which the tempo track can use as a guide for making tempo adjustments. This function could come in handy if, say, you wanted to set up a MIDI grid alongside an audio recording of a song that had a fluctuating tempo as opposed to a steady beat. This function can be a little tricky to work with, so be aware that it may take a lot of tweaking before you get a perfect tempo match.

> **NOTE**
>
> Because the tempo track is not covered in this book, I won't go into more detail on this function.

The Rest of the MIDI Menu

The next four entries in the MIDI menu are as follows:

- **Logical Editor and Logical Presets.** Both of these entries relate to the Logical editor, which is discussed in Chapter 11, "The List Editor, Logical Editor, and Project Browser."

- **Drum Map Setup.** This entry pertains to drum maps, covered in Chapter 10, "The Drum Editor."

- **Insert Velocities.** If this sounds familiar, it's because you learned about insert velocity in Chapter 3, "The Toolbar." Selecting this entry in the MIDI menu simply offers a fancier way to work with the insert velocities and setup feature, as shown in Figure 5.12. Notice that the number configuration is exactly the same as the list in the toolbar's Insert Velocity display; the only real difference is that this dialog box has some handy little sliders, meaning you can use your mouse to scroll up or down through the velocity range.

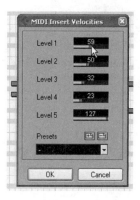

Figure 5.12

The "fancy" MIDI Insert Velocities dialog box.

Just below the Insert Velocities entry on the MIDI menu is the Reset option. You might be thinking that selecting this option would "reset" your system, deleting everything you've been working on, causing you to have to start all over again from the beginning—much like an operation such as a *factory reset*, which can be found on many of today's synths. This Reset option, however, is not a factory reset. Instead, selecting the MIDI menu's Reset option puts an end to the stuck MIDI notes you may occasionally experience due to a malfunction of sorts. Specifically, selecting this option sends a MIDI off message on all notes and MIDI channels. This MIDI off message isn't recorded and won't affect your sequence or edit in any way; it's simply designed to kill that evil MIDI demon whenever it rears its ugly head! Hopefully you won't have to use the Reset option often, but if you do, you'll be glad it's there. The important thing to know about it is that it won't hurt your recording.

6

Working with MIDI in the Project Window

Even though you're halfway through this book, you've barely scratched the surface of Cubase. For one thing, everything you've done so far has been in the Key editor. Don't let this scare you! You've already learned almost everything you need to know to enjoy a great MIDI editing experience in Cubase.

When you start a new project (or song) in Cubase, it is not created in the Key editor. Instead, it is opened in the project window. If you've already used Cubase a bit, chances are you spent the majority of your time in the project window; it provides an overview of the entire song you're working on. In it, you can see all the MIDI tracks and audio tracks at once. It's the place to be if you want to make dramatic, large-scale changes to your song—that is, changes that occur on the measures level rather than the notes level. For example, if you want to cut out a verse, you do it in the project window. Likewise, if you want to repeat a four-measure loop, the project window makes it a lot easier than the other Cubase editors.

> **NOTE**
>
> The reason I started you out using the Key editor rather than the project window is that I wanted to get you going right in the heart of where most detailed MIDI editing takes place. When working with MIDI in Cubase, you'll spend most of your time in either the project window or the Key editor.

The project window can be used for many Cubase tasks, but in this book, you'll focus primarily on how it relates to MIDI and MIDI editing. Start by opening Song7 from this book's CD-ROM in the project window. Right off the bat, you'll probably notice that there are a lot of differences between the Key editor and the project window. One of the main differences is in the toolbar—specifically, many of the tools available in the Key editor's toolbar are not available in the project window. That's because you're a little more limited when editing MIDI in the project window. Although only a few of the tools available in the Key editor are present in the project window, there are several tools in the project window that are *not* available in the Key editor. To see a list of available tools in the project window, right-click the toolbar (see Figure 6.1).

Figure 6.1

The project window's toolbar display setup menu.

A quick glance at the tools listed reveals that you're familiar with only five of them: Tool Buttons, Nudge Palette, Autoscroll, Snap/Quantize, and Color Menu. Before you get overwhelmed by the number of tools you haven't explored yet, allow me to ease your worries. Of the remaining 10 tools, two have nothing to do with MIDI, another two are quite simple, and the remaining six are duplicates of tools featured on the transport. It makes sense, then, to discuss the various transport tools first.

The Transport Tools

To see the available transport tools, right-click anywhere on the transport (see Figure 6.2). You'll probably notice some similarities between what's listed here and what you saw in the toolbar display setup menu—specifically, Performance, Locators, Main Transport, Play Order, and Marker entries. That's because these five tools are basically the same tools as the performance meter, locators, transport buttons, play order controls, and markers tools found in the list on the toolbar, with a few subtle differences (which I'll point out as we go). Cubase gives you an option of showing these tools on the transport or on the toolbar. To show them on the transport, choose Show All in the list. Your transport should appear as in Figure 6.3.

> **NOTE**
>
> One great thing about using these tools from the transport is that they're available even when you're working in other editors. This differs from toolbar buttons, which differ according to what window or editor you're using. Plus, the transport can display all the tools at once, even when you use a single-monitor setup.

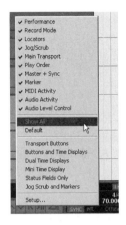

Figure 6.2

The transport control's menu display setup menu, showing the available tools.

Figure 6.3

The transport "showing it all."

Performance/Performance Meter

The purpose of the performance tool, which is roughly equivalent to the toolbar's performance meter and is located on the far left side of the transport (see Figure 6.4), is to monitor the performance of your computer system while it's running Cubase and all its plug-ins. It has two vertical LED-type displays, with the display on the left revealing CPU performance and the display on the right showing hard-drive performance.

Figure 6.4

The transport's performance meter.

Using MIDI alone will not trigger either one of these displays because MIDI is pretty lightweight for most of today's computers. What *will* trigger these displays, especially the CPU performance meter, is the use of VST instruments and other plug-ins, most of which require a great deal of processing power to operate. The more of these you run, the more you'll notice the left display climbing. As for the display on the right, it mostly reflects how your audio recordings are being processed, but it also reflects how many VST samplers are operating because most VST samplers pull the samples directly from the hard drive.

> **TIP**
>
> There are many ways to resolve overheating your system. One of the easiest is to bounce down VST instrument tracks so that they become audio tracks; another is to freeze your VST instrument tracks. I won't be getting into the details on this subject in this book, but you can find information in the Cubase manual to help you resolve any performance issues you may experience.

In addition to using the performance meter on the toolbar or transport, you can also pull up a performance meter in its own window by pressing the F12 key on your keyboard or by opening the Devices menu in the menu bar and selecting VST Performance (see Figure 6.5).

Figure 6.5
The VST Performance window.

Locators

The left and right *locators* determine the start and end points of a song, respectively, and are there to help you as you work on the grid. When the transport is in Cycle mode, Cubase continuously loops the *work area*, or everything between the left and right locators and indicated by a blue ruler. In Song7, the work area is between measures 5 and 25 (see Figure 6.6).

Figure 6.6
The left and right locators and the work area.

The Locators displays on the toolbar and transport are numerical displays that indicate the location of the left and right locators on the ruler. For example, as shown in Figure 6.7, Song7's left locator is set to 5.1.1.0, and its right locator is set to 25.1.1.0. The first decimal in each entry represents the measure, the second decimal refers to the beat, and the next two decimals are further divisions of the beat within the measure. By changing the numbers in the transport's or toolbar's Locators display, you also change the positions of the left and right locators on the ruler. The Locators display also enables you to jump your cursor to the position of the left or right locator by clicking L or R, respectively. The difference between the transport's Locators display and the toolbar's is that the transport's display also includes the following features, which are handy primarily for recording and overdubbing:

- **Punch In button.** When this button is activated, recording will not begin until the cursor passes the left locator.

- **Punch Out button.** When this button is activated, recording will stop when the cursor passes the right locator (although playing will continue until the track has been stopped).

- **Pre-Roll field.** The value in this field refers to the place in the track where the recording will start before the left locator. It's meant to protect you from missing a pickup into a measure or some other last-minute inspired performance noodlings.

- **Post-Roll field.** Use this field to specify the point after the right locator at which recording should stop. It's great for those notes that keep on going.

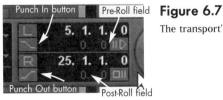

Figure 6.7

The transport's Locators display.

Main Transport/Transport Buttons

If you've ever used a tape recorder, you should be familiar with these buttons. In case you're not, Figure 6.8 outlines which one is which. The difference between the transport's buttons and the equivalent buttons on the toolbar is that the toolbar contains no fast-forward or rewind button. In truth, the only reason I can see to use the transport buttons on the toolbar is if you're working with several open windows and the transport gets lost behind them. Having the option of using these transport buttons on the toolbar ensures you always have easy access to them.

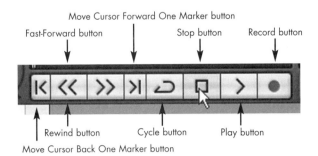

Figure 6.8

The transport buttons.

> **NOTE**
>
> As mentioned earlier, when the Cycle button is activated, a continuous loop is created between the left and right locators. As for the buttons relating to markers, you'll learn about those in the next section.

Marker/Markers

Markers are points you can set up so that you can easily move your cursor to specific locations on the ruler. If you're "old school" like I am, you can think of using markers as being sort of like setting up locate points on a tape machine. Using markers can make your editing a lot faster. The transport's marker display has 15 markers points and a Show Markers button (see Figure 6.9). Clicking this button launches a special Markers dialog box, shown in Figure 6.10.

> **NOTE**
>
> Unlike the markers display on the transport, the markers display on the toolbar does not have a Show Markers button, and it limits you to using only 10 markers instead of 15.

Figure 6.9
The transport's marker display.

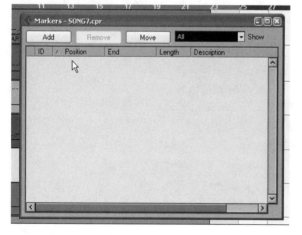

Figure 6.10
The Markers dialog box.

There are a couple of ways to add markers. One is by placing the cursor at the position where you want the marker and clicking the Markers dialog box's Add button. The other way is to place the cursor where you'd like the marker and press the Alt key on your keyboard while selecting a number from the marker display on the transport. To remove a marker, just select the marker in the Marker dialog box and click the Remove button. If you need to adjust the position of a marker, you can do so either by opening the Markers dialog box, double-clicking and entering a new numerical value in the marker's time display in the Position column, or moving the cursor to the correct point, selecting the marker in the Marker dialog box, and clicking the Move button. If you're playing back a track and you want the cursor to jump to a marker, simply click the corresponding number in the display box, and the cursor will move to that location.

> **NOTE**
>
> A special type of marker, called a *cycle marker*, can be set up on what's called the *marker track*. This involves working with song sections and cycle editing, which relate less to MIDI editing than to the editing of a song. For this reason, this book does not discuss the cycle marker or the marker track.

Play Order/Play Order Controls

The play order controls, shown in Figure 6.11, are used for creating a map of song parts or sections, making them handy for those who prefer to think of a song as sections as opposed to one continuous piece. Because these controls are in no way specific to MIDI editing, I won't cover them further except to note that there is no real difference between the controls on the toolbar and the ones on the transport.

Figure 6.11

The play order controls.

Other Transport Controls

There are several other very important features on the transport, particularly with regard to recording. Unfortunately, because they don't relate specifically to MIDI editing, I won't go over them in this book—with the exception of two: the time display and the MIDI input signal indicator.

The Time Display

Even though the time display, shown in Figure 6.12, is not listed in the transport's display setup menu, it's always present on the transport. As you can see, this display consists of two different times: a primary and a secondary. Both represent the exact location of the cursor but can show it in different time formats. For example, you could have one display set to show the cursor's location in bars and beats and the other display set to show the cursor's position in minutes and seconds.

Clicking the icon just to the right of either time display reveals a drop-down list, from which you can select various time-display options. Changing the primary time display also changes the ruler's time reference. If you need to change the position of the cursor, you can adjust the time display numerically, and the cursor will follow. Just to the left of the primary time display are plus (+)

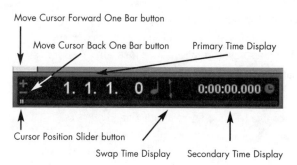

Figure 6.12

The transport's time display.

Move Cursor Forward One Bar button

Move Cursor Back One Bar button   Primary Time Display

Cursor Position Slider button

Swap Time Display   Secondary Time Display

and minus (–) buttons; clicking the plus button moves the cursor forward one bar, while clicking the minus button moves it back one bar. To swap your primary and secondary time displays, click the symbol located between the two displays. One of the handiest tools on the transport's time display is the cursor position slider, located just below the primary time display. By clicking and dragging this slider, you can position the cursor wherever you need it with very little effort.

> **NOTE**
>
> The time display on the toolbar does not include the plus and minus buttons, nor does it have the handy cursor position slider. Finally, it does not include the drop-down lists for selecting different time-display options.

The MIDI Input Signal Indicator

If you use a MIDI keyboard for your editing, you'll want to know about the MIDI input signal indicator, located just to the right of the markers display on the transport (see Figure 6.13). This simple display enables you to make sure you are receiving a MIDI signal into your computer. This comes in handy if you aren't getting any sound; you can check your MIDI signal to determine whether the problem is a MIDI problem or an audio concern.

Figure 6.13

Receiving MIDI loud and clear!

> **NOTE**
>
> Located just to the right of the MIDI input signal indicator is the audio input signal indicator, which serves the same purpose as the MIDI input signal indicator, but for audio.

More New Toolbar Buttons

Now that you've gotten through a significant portion of that intimidating new toolbar menu, it's time to tackle the remaining four toolbar features that are new to you: the Activate Project button, the Constrain Delay Compensation button, the view switches, and the automation mode tools.

The Activate Project Button

Located in the top-left corner of the project window's toolbar is the Activate Project button, which displays a circle with a small line through the top of it (see Figure 6.14). The main purpose of this button, which is always present on the project window's toolbar, is to select a specific project when you have several projects open at the same time.

Figure 6.14

The Activate Project button.

> **NOTE**
>
> Although Cubase can play back only one project at a time, it can have several projects open at once. When you have several projects open, you can move objects from one project to another, which can come in very handy.

The Constrain Delay Compensation Button

Assuming you have opted to select it in the toolbar display menu, the Constrain Delay Compensation button, shown in Figure 6.15, is just to the right of the Activate Project button. This button's sole purpose is to correct sync issues between recorded audio tracks and VST instruments. I look at it as a panic button, something you need to use only when you're having sync issues.

Figure 6.15

The Constrain Delay Compensation button.

The View Switches

The five buttons to the right of the Constrain Delay Compensation button are called the *view switches* (see Figure 6.16). They're used to show or hide five displays in the project window: the inspector, the Info Line, the overview, the pool, and the mixer.

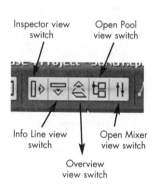

Inspector view switch
Open Pool view switch
Info Line view switch
Open Mixer view switch
Overview view switch

Figure 6.16

The view switches.

The Inspector Switch

Activating the first of these switches reveals a large info box for the selected track, just to the left of the track display (see Figure 6.17). This tool, called the inspector, is very useful when you need to take a closer look at what's happening behind each track. It is also good for making changes to the entire track. You'll go over the inspector's functions when you take a closer look at a MIDI track, a little later in this chapter.

The Info Line Switch

Remember the Info Line in the Key editor? This is the same thing, except it displays information for parts instead of notes. When you activate the Info Line view switch, which looks like the Show Info Line button in the Key editor, a line of information about the selected part in the part display appears just under the toolbar (see Figure 6.18). This information includes the following:

■ **Name.** Click in this field and type a new name to change the name of the selected part.

■ **Start, End, and Length.** Changing the values in any of these fields, either by typing over the existing value or using the arrows located next to a field to adjust the value, changes the position of the part, just as clicking in the corresponding fields in the Key editor affects a note.

- **Offset.** The Offset field enables you to change the position of the events within the part in relation to where the part starts.

- **Mute.** To mute a part, you can either use the Mute tool or change the value in this Mute field to mute.

- **Lock.** This is a safety feature and can be very useful. When you lock a part, you are protecting it from being edited accidentally. Note that it protects only the selected part.

- **Transpose.** This field offers a quick way to alter the pitch of the selected part, either up or down on the chromatic scale.

- **Velocity.** Changing this field works very much like choosing the Add/Subtract type in the Velocity dialog box, accessible from the MIDI menu. By raising or lowering the value, you raise or lower the velocity of every event within the part, without changing the difference of the velocity between each of the events within the part.

Figure 6.17

The inspector.

NOTE

When making changes in the Info Line, it's important to remember that the changes affect the whole selected part, as opposed to certain notes or events within the selected part.

Figure 6.18

The project window's Info Line.

The Overview Switch

Clicking the Overview view switch, located just to the right of the Info Line view switch, opens another line display just above the track and part display (see Figure 6.19). The information in this line is simply a dramatically zoomed-out view of the part display. This is another handy way of helping you change the view of the part display within your screen. Using the overview is also a good way to manage your view while working in the project window; trying to see an entire project (especially with a single monitor setup) is quite a task in itself.

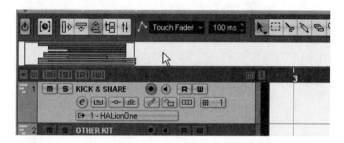

Figure 6.19

The overview display.

To use the overview display, click and drag with the OST to create a box similar to the multiple objects selection box over the parts displayed in the overview. The box, outlined with a solid blue line, represents the parts that will be displayed in your part display window. After you have created a box, you can resize it using the OST's arrow tool. As you resize it, notice how your large view of the parts display changes its zoom. When the box is the desired size, move the OST over the blue outlined box in the overview display and notice the tiny hand that appears (see Figure 6.20). You can use this tiny hand to move the display box to the left or right in the overview, enabling you to find the exact view you require as you work within the part display. When the OST is not over the overview display, the tiny hand vanishes.

Figure 6.20

The overview's "tiny hand" on the display "box."

The Open Pool and the Open Mixer Switches

Although the next two switches are very useful for working in Cubase, they are not relevant to MIDI editing. The switch located just to the right of the Overview switch is the Open Pool switch; click it to open the Cubase pool, a handy tool for managing the audio files (and video files) used in your project. The switch just to the right of the Open Pool switch is the Open Mixer switch; you click it to open the mixer. Everything runs through the mixer, including VST instruments, audio tracks, and effects. Automation happens with the mixer as well. That said, although the mixer can be a very handy tool, you can mix a song (even with automation) without actually using it. And even though there are MIDI functions in the mixer, those function aren't relevant to MIDI editing in Cubase.

The Automation Mode Tools

To the right of the switch buttons on the toolbar are the *automation mode* tools (see Figure 6.21). The main purpose of these tools is for working with automated mixing in Cubase. Even though you can use the automation to control MIDI functions, and technically, you can edit your automation, this goes just a few steps beyond what you need to know to edit MIDI in Cubase. That said, the automation mode tools are very useful, and I hope you will take the time to learn about what they can do for you from the Cubase manual or from other technical guides.

Figure 6.21

The automation mode tools.

NOTE

In addition to the zoom tools in the lower-right corner of the display, there is also a small vertical zoom slider on the right side of the screen, closer to the top of the part display, in the project window. This slider is for changing the view of the events or audio within a part. You can also increase or reduce the height of each track in a manner similar to how you adjusted the controller lanes' height. Both of these additional zooms can be very useful tools when working in the project window.

"Changed" Tools

Finally, you're ready to turn to the project window's tool buttons; this time, however, things look a little different than they did in the Key editor. Right away you'll probably notice that there are three new tool buttons, one tool is missing, and the OST has a drop-down menu (see Figure 6.22).

Changes in the OST

As mentioned, one of the more obvious differences between the tool buttons in the Key editor and those in the project window is that the OST tool button includes a drop-down menu. Try

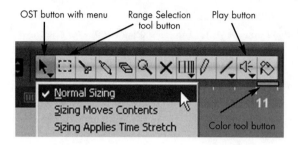

OST button with menu   Range Selection   Play button
                           tool button

Color tool button

Figure 6.22

The "changed" tool buttons in the project window, with the OST's menu open.

clicking the down arrow on the button to view the menu. You'll see that it offers access to three modes of sizing with the OST within the project window's part display: Normal Sizing, Sizing Moves Contents, and Sizing Applies Time Stretch.

Normal Sizing

When the drop-down list's first option, Normal Sizing, is selected, the OST uses the same basic selection and sizing methods as it did in the Key editor when used with notes in the Note display. Note that when you use the OST to change the size of the part, the part may get bigger or smaller, but the notes and events within the part do not move or change. Here's a quick walk-through:

1. Click the down arrow on the OST tool button and choose Normal Sizing from the menu that appears.

2. Using the zoom tools in the bottom-right corner of the screen, zoom in on track 1 to the part labeled "kick & snare," which starts at measure 7. Notice the little line and dash markings on the track; they represent the notes within the part.

3. Place the OST over the small white box in the bottom-left corner of the part. Notice how the OST cursor changes to a double-sided arrow.

4. Click and drag the arrow to resize the part so that it starts at measure 5 instead of measure 7 (see Figure 6.23). Notice that the notes do not change position within the part, even though the part has been lengthened by two measures.

5. Play back the track. You will not hear any difference.

6. With Normal Sizing still selected, use the OST to restore the kick & snare part to its original state.

Sizing Moves Contents

The drop-down list's second sizing option is Sizing Moves Contents. The difference between this method of sizing and the Normal method is that when you resize the part, the notes actually change positions along with the part.

Figure 6.23

The OST changes the part length without affecting the notes within the part.

This method can get a little tricky, so let's give it a run through. Begin by repeating the steps in the previous exercise, but this time choosing Sizing Moves Contents in step 1. Notice that instead of staying in place, the notes move to the start of measure 5 along with the part—meaning that the rest of the notes in the part follow. As you can see in Figure 6.24, this throws off the sync of the kick & snare part with the other tracks. Play back the track, noticing how the kick & snare part starts and ends earlier. Then, with Sizing Moves Contents still selected, use the OST to restore the kick & snare part to its original state, with the start of the part once again at measure 7.

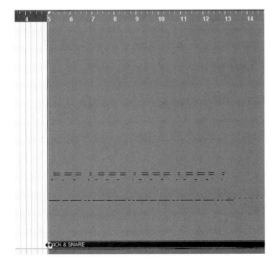

Figure 6.24

Using the OST's Sizing Moves Contents setting.

Sizing Applies Time Stretch

The third option in the OST's drop-down list, Sizing Applies Time Stretch, can be the trickiest of all. When using this setting, the notes don't just simply move with the part; instead, the part *stretches* the notes so they maintain the same relative difference in time amongst each other but cover the length of the newly resized part. This in turn creates its own tempo inside the individual part, which can throw notes completely off the grid when it comes to quantizing. To get the hang of it, repeat the steps in the preceding two sections, this time choosing Sizing Applies Time Stretch from the drop-down list; when you're finished, listen to the part. Sounds pretty messed up, doesn't it?

You might reasonably wonder why on Earth anyone wants to use either of these last two methods to resize MIDI parts. Keep in mind that this type of resizing isn't limited to MIDI parts; it can also be applied to audio parts. In some cases, this type of movement can actually make a part that doesn't quite fit the grid snap to it with just a little tweaking. It can also be used to create a tempo-change effect during a song. Even though the first option, Normal Sizing, is the more commonly used one, you could get into some pretty creative editing using the other methods.

The Range Selection Tool Button

Next to the OST is a fancy new tool that looks like a dotted-line box: the Range Selection tool. Although you can use the OST to select multiple objects by clicking and dragging, Cubase added the Range Selection tool to the project window to make selecting multiple objects a little easier. This tool works just like the OST with the multiple selection box except it creates a light-blue shaded box over the selected parts that doesn't disappear when you let go of the mouse button. In fact, when you *do* let go of the mouse button, you can resize the selection area just as you would resize a part with the OST.

The Play Button

Moving across the row of tool buttons, you'll see the familiar Split tool, Glue tool, Erase tool, Zoom tool, Mute tool, Time Warp tool, Draw tool, and Line tool. In the project window, these tools function with parts the same way they do in the Key Editor with notes. The only slight difference is that the Line tool no longer offers the Paint option in its drop-down menu, and the Trim tool is no longer available.

Just past the Line tool is a button that resembles the Audio Feedback button on the Key editor's toolbar. Here, however, it's called the Play button—although it has a similar purpose. If, after selecting the Play button, you click and hold the mouse button on a part, the part plays back from where the speaker pointer is positioned on the part.

There are two ways to use the Play button, and you can choose the method you want from the button's drop-down list:

■ **Play.** The Play option plays back the track at the tempo of your song.

■ **Scrub.** The Scrub option acts sort of like an old-school tape deck or turntable, allowing you to "turn off the motor" and manually "roll the tape across the heads." In this way, you can hear the sound of the part in the right order without having to be restricted to a tempo of any kind. Using the Scrub setting while working with audio, you can sound like a DJ working the wheels of steel. Keep in mind, though, that MIDI responds differently because it's triggering the sound instead of playing a recording of a sound.

The Color and Color Selector Tool Buttons

The Color tool button is next to the Play button and features a paint bucket. You generally use this tool in conjunction with the Color Selector tool, located on the right-most side of the toolbar. Here's how:

1. Click the down arrow on the Color Selector tool button and select any one of the 16 available colors (or create your own color) from the drop-down list that appears. The color you choose appears both on the selected part in the project window and just under the Color tool button.

2. Click the Color tool button to select it.

3. Click on a part. The part is colored with the selected hue.

4. Repeat as needed. This is an excellent way to group parts and help avoid confusion.

The Snap and Quantize Display

Moving across the toolbar, past the tool buttons, you'll see the Nudge buttons (minus the four Transpose buttons). These six buttons move parts in the same way the first six Nudge buttons in the Key editor moved notes. Located next to the Nudge buttons is the Auto Scroll button, which functions identically to the Key editor's Auto Scroll button.

Just past the Auto Scroll button are other familiar tools: the Snap button, the Snap Type selector, and the Quantize display, all of which are the same here as in the project window—except you have one more option: the Grid Type display. The Grid Type display enables you to snap your parts to the nearest bar, beat, or whatever unit is shown in the quantize display. To change its setting, just select from the display's drop-down menu, as shown in Figure 6.25.

Figure 6.25
The Grid Type display's drop-down menu.

The last unfamiliar tool, and the least of your MIDI editing worries, is the Snap to Zero Crossing tool, which looks like a crosshair slashed by a diagonal line (see Figure 6.26). This button is used when merging audio parts so that the parts don't create pops. It's a very nice tool button, but completely unrelated to MIDI.

Figure 6.26
The Snap to Zero Crossing button.

MIDI Tracks and the Inspector

You may already be somewhat familiar with MIDI tracks in Cubase, but because there are some very important MIDI functions that you can control from the track and the inspector, I thought it was important to go over them here. The MIDI track can display as many as 18 buttons or fields, some of which are duplicated in the inspector. In contrast, the inspector has so many accessible functions that Cubase had to divide it into eight different function groups! I'm going to be as brief as possible, but I want to touch on all of these functions because they are important.

The MIDI Track

For a brief explanation of the functions on a MIDI track, see Figure 6.27 and the numbered list that follows.

> **NOTE**
>
> If you can't see all 18 buttons and fields in your project window, right-click the track and choose Track Controls Settings. In the dialog box that opens, you can set up the controls in the way you want them displayed, much like setting up the toolbar or transport display.

1. **Mute.** When this button is enabled, the entire track is silenced.
2. **Solo.** When this button is enabled, all tracks are silenced except those that are soloed.

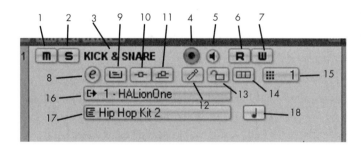

Figure 6.27
A close-up of the MIDI track.

3. **Name.** Taking the time to name your tracks can really help you later. Just click in the Name field and type away. The field is limited to a preset number of characters, but you can change this number by resetting the Length parameter of the Name field located under the visible controls column in the Track Controls Settings menu.

4. **Record Enable.** This button needs to be activated if you want to record on the track. If you don't want to record on the track, make sure the button is *dis*abled!

5. **Monitor.** Activating this button enables you to hear the input signal in monitoring. This comes in handy if you're using external synths and are monitoring through Cubase.

6. **Read Enable.** Activating this button enables Cubase to read automation that has been written on this track.

7. **Write Enable.** Activating this button enables you to record automation for anything that can be automated in Cubase.

8. **Edit Channel Settings.** Click this button to see the Edit Channel Settings dialog box shown in Figure 6.28, which provides a lot more controls to work with.

9. **Edit In-Place.** Clicking this button changes the track into a mini-Key editor. You'll learn more about it in Chapter 7, "The In-Place Editor and the Edit Menu."

10. **Inserts State.** Use this on/off button for any insert effects you may be using on the track. You'll learn more about using inserts in Chapter 9, "Working with MIDI Effects and Modifiers."

11. **Sends State.** Use this on/off button for any send effects you may be using on the track. For more information about send effects, see Chapter 9.

12. **Drum Map.** This on/off button enables you to record your drum track to a preset drum map. For more details, see Chapter 10, "The Drum Editor."

13. **Lock.** Much like the part lock located in the Info Line, this is a safety feature for the entire track.

14. **Lane Display Type.** This handy feature allows you to display several takes or parts on the same track at the same time. These parts can be treated just as any other part on any other track would be; the only difference is they are separated into tracks within the track, called *lanes*. There are three options in displaying your lanes:

   ■ **Lanes Off.** Choosing this setting means only one part will be displayed at a time.

- ■ **Auto.** If this setting is chosen, Cubase positions the lanes wherever it wants to.

- ■ **Fixed.** Choosing this setting means that after you've determined a place for the lane, it will hold its position in the track.

15. **Channel.** This indicates which MIDI channel will be playing back the part (1–16).

16. **Output.** This field displays output information. The signal can be sent to a MIDI output from your computer that may be going to an external synth, or it can be sent to a VST instrument that is currently loaded and activated in Cubase. Without having your output properly set up, you won't be able to hear the instrument played back.

17. **Program.** This field takes the output information one step farther by actually naming the instrument program or patch you are using on your VST instrument.

18. **Toggle Time Base.** This button enables you to switch between recording in the usual musical mode, in which MIDI time is recorded in bars and beats, and linear mode, which uses time as a reference. When using linear mode, tempo adjustments in the tempo track or on the transport do not affect the MIDI recording.

As mentioned, clicking the Edit Channel Settings button on the MIDI track opens the Edit Channel Settings dialog box. For an explanation of the settings in this dialog box, see Figure 6.28 and the numbered list that follows. (Note that everything relating to inserts and sends will be covered in finer detail in Chapter 9.)

NOTE

Many of the settings found in the Edit Channel Settings dialog box are duplicated in the inspector.

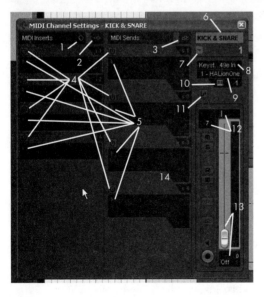

Figure 6.28

The Edit Channel Settings dialog box.

1. **Preset Management.** This enables you to store one or a group of insert effects and their settings under a name, which you can create and recall when needed.

2. **Shows Active Inserts.** This indicates when inserts have been activated by appearing highlighted in blue.

3. **Shows Active Sends.** This indicates when sends have been activated by appearing highlighted in blue.

4. **Activate Inserts/Sends.** This powers an insert or send on or off.

5. **Select Effect Type.** This displays a list of all the MIDI effects available from which you can choose which effect you'd like to use.

6. **Channel Name.** This displays what channel (track) you are currently working with. You can edit the name by clicking in its field.

7. **Choose Edit Channel.** There is not one Edit Channel Settings display dialog box for every channel; instead, they all share one display. You use this button to toggle between different channels. Note that the number represents the track number and is not to be confused with a MIDI channel.

8. **MIDI Input.** Select the source of your MIDI signal here.

9. **MIDI Output and MIDI Channel.** These are identical to the controls by the same name located on the MIDI track. Remember that you have the option to remove this from the MIDI track if you like.

10. **Open Device.** This is used to access your VST instrument's edit panel.

11. **Input Transformer.** This is an on/off button for the input transformer, which is discussed in more detail in Chapter 12, "The Score Editor."

12. **Pan.** You can use this to set the MIDI stereo imaging of the selected sound. This can also be automated.

13. **Volume.** This is a MIDI volume control for the selected instrument—not to be confused with the audio volume of the selected instrument.

14. **Mute, Solo, Read, Write, Inserts and Sends State, Monitor, and Record Enable.** These are duplicates of the controls on the MIDI track.

A Closer Look at the Inspector

Like the toolbar, the Info Line, and the track display, the inspector has its own setup dialog box. To access it, right-click the upper part of the inspector while the inspector is open to the left of the track display.

This dialog box lists seven display setups, along with a MIDI Track Control that's set up by default. These display setups are as follows: the MIDI Modifiers, MIDI Inserts, MIDI Sends, MIDI Fader,

Notepad, User Panel, and Instrument. Before you continue, make sure that all seven of these display setups are checked in the setup dialog box.

The MIDI Track Control

Most of controls in the inspector's MIDI Track Control menu are simply duplicate controls from the track display and the Edit Channel Settings dialog box. Having the controls here just gives you even more ways to display them the way you'd like. There are, however, three noticeable differences, including one new control. These are as follows (see Figure 6.29):

> **NOTE**
>
> You may have noticed already, but when you click the track name in the inspector's MIDI Track Control menu, you can name or rename a track. Most of the time, when a name is displayed in Cubase, you can click the Name field and change the name.

Figure 6.29

The inspector's MIDI Track Control menu.

- **Fader.** This is very similar to the fader found in the Edit Channel Settings dialog box. The only real difference is that it's horizontal, and it takes up less space on your window because it's no frills.

- **Pan.** Cubase has provided another pan (which is very similar to the one in the Edit Channel Settings dialog box) to match the simple fader above. This time it creates a blue line from its zero point to its pan setting.

■ **Track delay.** This setting allows you to position the entire track either forward or backward in time (milliseconds) in relation to the rest of the tracks. This is a great tool for correcting an unwanted MIDI delay or easily creating delay effects without actually using any sort of processor.

The MIDI Modifiers Menu

You can open only one of the inspector's menus at a time, so click MIDI Modifiers. The MIDI Track Control menu folds back into the inspector, and the MIDI Modifiers menu is displayed, as in Figure 6.30. Much of what you see may look familiar, but there are some new goodies to play with, too. You'll learn a lot more about MIDI modifiers in Chapter 9.

Figure 6.30

The inspector's MIDI Modifiers menu.

The MIDI Inserts Menu

Opening the inspector's MIDI Inserts menu reveals a setup that looks very much like what you found in the Edit Channel Settings dialog box (see Figure 6.31). You'll be taking a closer look at this in Chapter 9.

The MIDI Sends Menu

Opening the inspector's MIDI Sends menu, you can see that the sends from the Edit Channel Settings dialog box are duplicated in the inspector (see Figure 6.32).

Figure 6.31

The inspector's MIDI Inserts menu.

Figure 6.32

The inspector's MIDI Sends menu.

The MIDI Fader Menu

Opening the inspector's MIDI Fader menu reveals yet another fader with controls very similar to the fader found in the Edit Channel Settings dialog box. The only difference here is that the fader has numbers along its left side that you can use to activate and deactivate your channel inserts and sends (see Figure 6.33).

Figure 6.33

The inspector's MIDI fader and its insert and send activation buttons.

> **NOTE**
>
> To make some fine incremental numerical adjustments to the volume when using a fader, just click in the number field located under the fader and adjust the numbers up or down with a mouse wheel or by typing the exact volume you're looking for.

The MIDI Notepad Display

Since the words "MIDI," "note," and "pad" are use very commonly in music, I can see how you could get a little confused here. It would be nice if you could type in a few words here and have your synth play a nice, soothing vocoder synth pad with your phrase, but unfortunately this tool does nothing of the sort. It's simply a virtual "sticky note" that you can use to leave little reminders to yourself about whatever you want. The only difference is you stick these to your MIDI tracks instead of to your fridge (see Figure 6.34).

The MIDI User Panel Display

Imagine if you could control every parameter in your external synth from Cubase. Now stop imagining; I'll tell you how you can do it. It's going to take a little work and some research, but Cubase gives you the power to create virtual controls for the parameters on your external synths. You can actually open those controls from this little user panel within the inspector (see Figure 6.35). The trick is you have to first build the control panel map in Cubase; then you can load it into this user

Figure 6.34

The inspector's "sticky note" for MIDI tracks.

panel. To access your pre-made control maps, just click the down arrow on the panel to reveal your panel folder.

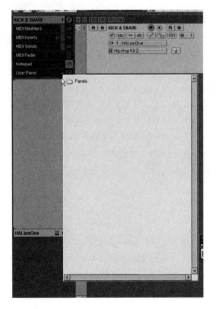

Figure 6.35

The MIDI user panel.

TIP

To read more about the user panel, open the Help menu and choose Documentation (in Acrobat PDF format), then open the "MIDI Devices and Features" document. It gets a little on the technical side, but if you really want to get the most out of your external synth, this could come in very handy.

The Instrument Display

Upon first glance, you'll notice that the inspector's MIDI Instrument menu contains the symbol that looks like the Open Device button in the Edit Channel Settings dialog box. Just as clicking that button in the Edit Channel Settings dialog box allows access to your VST instruments, so too does clicking the button here.

Located on the right side of the menu is an "e" symbol, again similar to the one in the Edit Channel Settings dialog box. Clicking this "e" brings up the audio instrument channel of the VST instrument; opening the menu itself gives you another whole menu for the audio instrumental channel settings for your instrument. Although this can be very useful, going into all the details about it here will be steering way off course. Just know that this is here and easy to access when you need to make audio changes that you can't make with MIDI (see Figure 6.36).

Figure 6.36

The inspector's MIDI Instrument menu and instrumental (audio) channel settings display.

7 The In-Place Editor and the Edit Menu

Now that you're familiar with the project window and its MIDI-editing capabilities, it's time to take it one step further in this chapter by exploring an editor that works along with the project window, called the In-Place editor. You'll find that it's very similar to an editor you already know how to use. This chapter also takes a look at the Edit menu, exploring what this menu has to offer in terms of MIDI editing.

Working with the In-Place Editor

To start this chapter off right, close any songs you may have open and open Song8 from the CD-ROM accompanying this book. With the song open, you will notice that you are in the project window but that one of the MIDI tracks is displayed differently from before. That's because the track is being displayed in the In-Place editor, which, as you can see, looks very much like a mini Key editor. There are a few differences between the In-Place editor and the Key editor, however. One is that, because you are still working within the project window, you are limited to using only the tools on the project windows toolbar. Another difference is that, because you are working in the project window, you can open the In-Place editor on several tracks at a time.

You zoom in and out on the In-Place editor vertically, the same way you expand and compress a MIDI track's width. After you have adjusted the width to how you like it, click anywhere in the In-Place editor's Note display and use your mouse wheel to roll the display up or down in pitch in order to view the desired range of notes.

Viewing controller lanes is a lot more limited in the In-Place editor than it is in the Key editor. Using the Controller Lane menu (located just below the keyboard on the left side), you will see that you have only a few viewing options from which to choose: showing no controller lanes, viewing all the *used* controller lanes, or viewing velocity only. The menu also enables you to save user presets for displaying the velocity lanes in these three ways so that you can specify which of the used controller lanes you would like to display, and so forth.

There are two ways to open the In-Place editor within the project window. The easiest way is to click the Open In-Place Editor button on the track display of the track you want to edit. The other is by first selecting the track you would like to edit and, from the MIDI menu, selecting Open In-Place Editor. Using either method, open the In-Place editor for the Funk Guitar track; it should look something like Figure 7.1 (depending on your zoom settings).

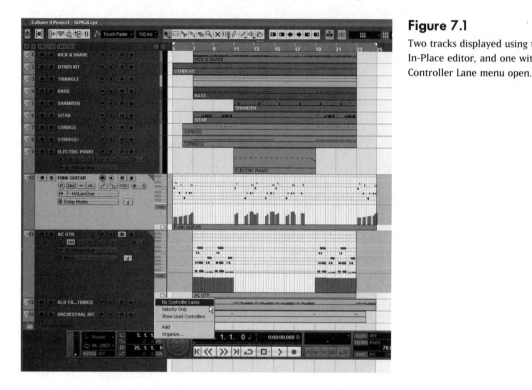

Figure 7.1

Two tracks displayed using the In-Place editor, and one with its Controller Lane menu open.

The important thing to remember about the In-Place editor is that you can use it to easily move notes from one part to another within the project window, or you can make a quick edit to a MIDI note while remaining in the project window. Another important thing to know is that not only can you access the Key editor from the project window by selecting Open Key Editor from the MIDI menu, you can also open the Key editor by simply double-clicking the part you want to edit.

The Edit Menu

At the top of the screen, just to the right of the File menu on the menu bar, is the Edit menu. Opening it, you'll see that it contains quite a list of edit commands, which you can use when you're editing MIDI or audio in Cubase (see Figure 7.2).

Figure 7.2
The Edit menu.

The "Oops! I Changed My Mind" Section

If you're human and make mistakes, you'll appreciate the first section of the Edit menu, which consists of three commands:

■ **Undo.** As is the case with many programs, clicking the Undo command enables you to step backward to the state of your song before your last edit. This can come in very handy, especially if you're like me and you like to play around with edits before you commit to one. If no edits have been made, the Undo command will not be accessible; if you have made edits, the command will appear as Undo *Last Edit* (i.e. Undo Move Note or Undo Delete Part).

■ **Redo.** The Redo command is just the opposite of the Undo command. Say you made an edit that you weren't sure you liked, so you undid it. After listening to the original, however, you decided you *did* like the edit. In that case, you can issue the Redo command in order to redo your edit. This is another handy command, although not quite as handy as Undo.

■ **History.** Clicking the History command opens a dialog box showing every edit you've made in this session since opening your song. If you want to undo all changes to a certain point in the song, use the line marker to pinpoint the spot to which you want to return and click OK; all of your edits up until that point will vanish. This is not much different from using Undo except that it's faster, especially if you want to undo a lot of edits.

CAUTION

The History dialog box does not enable you to remove a particular change you made several edits ago, leaving the subsequent edits intact. Your only option is to undo everything to the point where you made your mistake. From there, you'll have to perform your edits manually, as you did them the first time. This can be annoying if you did a lot of edits after the fact, so be warned!

The Edit Functions

Edit functions are found in the second and fourth sections of the Edit menu. Most of these functions can be accomplished in several ways, including using the commands listed next to them in the edit menu.

Cut, Copy, Paste, and Paste at Origin

To *cut* a part or event(s) is to remove it from the song, temporarily putting it on the Cubase *clipboard*, which holds the part until you are ready to paste it back into the song. To *paste* a part is to put the cut part into the song, most likely at a different location. *Copying* a part is similar to cutting a part, except the part is not removed from its original spot in the song; a copy of it is simply placed on the clipboard, from which it can then be pasted elsewhere in the song. To *paste at origin* simply means to paste a copy of the cut or copied part in the exact place from which it was cut or copied.

There are a few ways to cut, copy, and paste in Cubase. Here's one:

1. Using the OST, select the part(s) you want to cut or copy.

2. Open the Edit menu and choose Cut or Copy. (Remember that cutting a part will remove the original part from the song.)

3. Place the cursor at the point where you would like the part to be pasted back into the song.

4. Open the Edit menu and choose Paste. The part(s) will be pasted in at the cursor.

> **NOTE**
>
> My favorite editing commands are Copy and Paste. Indeed, it is this type of edit that has spawned a plethora of "two bar musicians"—that is, the kind of musician who doesn't have to be skilled enough to play like a virtuoso for the whole song, only good enough to play well for two bars, which can then be copied and pasted to create the rest of the song.

Although you can copy and paste the parts in this fashion all day long, in my opinion it's much easier to do it using the pro "click and drag" method, which bypasses the Edit menu altogether. Here's how:

1. Using the OST, select the part(s) you want to cut or copy.

2. To cut the part and paste it elsewhere in the song, click the part and drag it to its new location. If you want to copy the part rather than cut it, simply hold down the Alt key on your keyboard as you drag.

3. When the part is situated correctly, release the mouse button (and the Alt button). The part is cut or copied to the new location.

If you practice these steps a few times with different parts and groups of parts, you'll soon be the copy-and-paste master. I think you'll agree that this pro "click and drag" method makes a lot more sense than using the Edit menu functions.

> **NOTE**
>
> If you're experiencing déjà vu with regard to cutting and pasting parts, it's because cutting and pasting a part is basically the same as simply *moving* a part in a song. The main difference between cutting and pasting a part and moving a part is that when you move a part, it doesn't get copied to the clipboard first so that you can make more copies of the part you just moved. Moving a part is faster and easier than cutting and pasting if your objective is not to make multiple copies of a part. If your objective is to remove a part without pasting it elsewhere, then you'll find that using the Erase tool works better than using the Cut function.

Delete

The Delete function offers yet another way to erase a part or event from a song and operates in much the same way as the Erase tool. Simply select the part(s) you would like to remove, open the Edit menu, and choose Delete. You can also delete a part by selecting it and pressing the backspace or Delete key on your computer keyboard. This last way is quick, efficient, and just plain makes sense.

Split at Cursor and Split Loop

You've already learned how to split a note or part using the Split tool. The Split at Cursor and Split Loop commands are provided to make common split points easier. Split at Cursor splits parts where the cursor is positioned. To split certain parts only, those parts first need to be selected; otherwise, Split at Cursor splits all the parts. (To execute this command without opening the Edit menu, you can simply press Alt+X on your computer keyboard.) The Split Loop command works in a similar way, except that it creates two splits in the part(s)—one at the left locator's position and the other at the right locator's position. This is handy for creating that two-bar phrase (or whatever) that you want to copy and paste throughout the song.

Range

Selecting the Range command reveals a submenu of additional commands (see Figure 7.3):

- **Global Copy.** You use this command in much the same way you would copy a group of parts, except it copies only what is between the left and right locators.

- **Cut Time.** Using this command is similar to cutting a part, except that you first use the Range tool to select the part you want to cut. Then, after you execute the Cut Time command, the parts you selected are removed to the song and copied to the clipboard, and everything that was to the right of the cut parts is moved to the left to fill the gap. This could be a quick way to remove a chorus or verse from a song.

- **Delete Time.** This works similarly to Cut Time, except it doesn't move the selected range to the clipboard. Also, if you don't use the Range tool to select a range, Cubase assumes that whatever is between the left and right locators is the range.

- **Paste Time.** This command pastes the copied part into the song at the cursor's position. When a part is pasted into the song in this manner, any part that it's pasted over will remain in place but will be subservient to the newly pasted part, meaning it will be silent where the new part exists.

- **Paste Time at Origin.** This command works like the Paste Time command, but it automatically pastes the copied part into the song at the same place from which it was copied.

- **Split.** Using the Split command to split a selected range (that is, the blue selection box created with the Range tool) is similar to using the Split at Loop command. Just consider the start and end points of the selected range to be like the left and right locator points.

- **Crop.** When you crop a selected range (again using the Range tool), everything within the blue box remains in place, but everything that is *not* in the blue box is deleted. This is great for cutting off the start and end of a song. Keep in mind that *everything* that is not in the selected range will be deleted; this could be a drastic measure!

- **Insert Silence.** When you insert silence in the selected area, the selected area becomes nothing but space, with the parts or events that were within the selected area shifting to the right of the selected range's blue box.

While these little Range extras are great, sometimes the easiest way to perform these same tasks is to just use the OST, the Split tool, the Delete key, and the click-and-drag copy method.

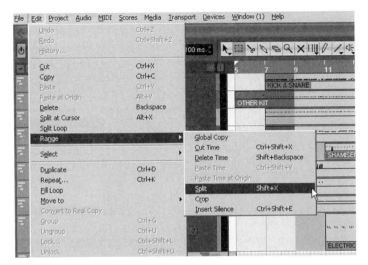

Figure 7.3

The Edit menu's Range submenu.

Duplicate, Repeat, and Fill Loop

Skipping over the Edit menu's Select section brings you to the remaining edit functions:

- **Duplicate.** Selecting a part or event and choosing Duplicate creates copy of the part, placing it just to the right of the original, selected part. This is ideal when you are working with a phrase or loop that you need to repeat one time.

- **Repeat.** If you are working with a loop or phrase that you want to repeat several times, select the loop or phrase and then choose the Edit menu's Repeat command. Doing so launches a dialog box that prompts you to specify how many times you want the selection to be duplicated. Enter the desired number of times and click OK; the number of duplicates you specified will be added to the right of the copied part.

- **Fill Loop.** This command works in a similar way but creates only enough duplicates to fill the space between the left and right locators. If the space is slightly shorter than the multiple copies can evenly fill, the last duplicate will extrude past the right locator for the rest of its length.

It's important to keep in mind that using any of these three duplication methods does *not* adjust the song in such a way that the parts to the right of the selected and duplicated parts are moved to make room. If the part is duplicated within the confines of other parts, the duplicate will appear over the old parts. Also, keep in mind that even though these three methods for duplicating a phrase work, the old standby click-and-drag method works almost as quickly (depending on how quickly you can perform the operation) and can usually help keep your work area from getting too messy if you use it appropriately.

Move To

The Move To command offers an alternative for moving part(s) without using the OST when making a common move. This command offers three types of moves:

- **Move to Cursor.** This is similar to the Paste at Cursor command, but instead of cutting and pasting the part to the cursor's location, it *moves* the part—which is essentially the same thing. The only difference is that when you move the part to the cursor, the part isn't first copied to the clipboard.

> **NOTE**
>
> Like in any menu, it's important to remember that when a command is disabled (that is, it appears grayed out in the menu), it means the command is not available for use. This might be because you're working with MIDI and the function applies to only audio, because the function does not operate in that particular editor, or simply because no part(s) has been selected to edit.

- **Move to Origin.** The Move to Origin command might seem pretty redundant, but if you've moved your part somewhere, and you just want to put it back where it came from, you can use this command. Keep in mind that you can also undo a move to return the part to its original location.
- **Move to Front and Move to Back.** The Move to Front and Move to Back commands only really work for parts that are overlapping. For example, if two parts are overlapping, you can use these commands to move the selected part so that it's on top of or beneath the other part. Keep in mind that this really only changes the *view* of the parts, so that you can see the events happening in the part that is being overlapped. It doesn't change the position of the events in any actual way.

Convert to Real Copy

This command is inactive because it's for audio only. When you copy an audio part, Cubase doesn't actually create a real copy of the audio file. Instead, it creates a *virtual copy* and plays back the original audio file. It's a very efficient way of handling audio files in Cubase, but occasionally you may find that you need a "real" audio copy so you can edit the copy without affecting the original source recording. Because this doesn't pertain to MIDI, I won't get into this in more detail; refer to your audio sources for more info.

Group and Ungroup

Grouping and ungrouping parts is a way of keeping parts organized when working in the project window. Think of parts as papers and of grouping the parts as being like putting a paper clip on several papers so that they stay together. When parts are grouped, they always stay together in their relative positions. If you select one of the grouped parts, the other parts in the group are selected as well. This works well for parts that always act together but are located on separate tracks. Once a group is selected, you can copy, split, move, or apply any other edit to it as a whole instead of to multiple tracks. When you are finished applying your edits, you can ungroup the parts to again work on each one separately.

Lock and Unlock

The Lock command works in the exact same way as the Lock function in the Info Line, except it doesn't give you multiple lock options in a drop-down menu. Instead, it locks the selected part(s) in the way that has been established in your Preferences setup. I'll touch on setting up your preferences in Chapter 13, "Now That You Know Everything There Is to Know About Editing MIDI in Cubase . . ." As you probably guessed, the Unlock command simply removes the safety lock.

Mute and Unmute

Mute and Unmute are yet more duplicate commands for operations you already know how to do. Specifically, you can use these commands to silence and un-silence parts the exact same way you would using the Mute tool or by selecting Mute from the Info Line in the project window.

Automatic Functions of the Edit Menu

Moving on to the next section, you come to three functions that you can enable or disable by checking or unchecking them on the menu:

- **Automation Follows Events.** When you're working with parts and automation, the automation is treated as a separate entity from the part and is placed in its own automation track. The Automation Follows Events function gives you the option to keep this automation track grouped. Like the Group and Ungroup commands, this makes it easier to work with parts and automation when parts are moved or edited within a song. If Automation Follows Events is on, then when the part moves, the automation moves with it in its relative place. If Automation Follows Events is off, then when a part is moved, the automation gets left in its original place, and the part acts separately from its automation. Sometimes it's necessary to group the two together, and sometimes it's necessary to ungroup them. It all depends on the song and the way in which you want to mix it.

- **Auto Select Events Under Cursor.** When Auto Select Events Under Cursor is enabled, all the events (including parts, notes, and so on) that the cursor touches will become selected on the selected tracks. That means while the song is playing back, the cursor will automatically select whatever it touches (on selected tracks only). Whenever the cursor has passed an

event in playback, that event will once again be deselected. This can be great if you're trying to pinpoint a note during playback; I think this feature works best in Scrub mode.

■ **Enlarge Selected Tracks.** With Enlarge Selected Tracks enabled, every time you select a
track or tracks, the track(s) expands its zoom vertically so that you can focus on that track
a little better. This is simply another way of automatically adjusting your view as you work.

More Zooming . . .

In case you are in need of even more ways to change your view in Cubase, you have another
whole menu dedicated just to that. Located just below the section with the automatic functions is
the Zoom command; clicking it opens a submenu with the following options:

■ **Zoom In and Zoom Out.** These do exactly what they say they do, using the cursor as the
centralized reference point. Each click zooms in or out one step.

■ **Zoom Full.** Clicking this widens your view so that the entire project is visible. This is a
quick and accurate way of getting the big picture.

■ **Zoom to Selection and Zoom to Selection (Horiz).** Clicking either of these options fills the
screen with whatever is currently selected. This is a quick way of getting right to the
details.

■ **Zoom to Event.** This option is available only in the audio sample editor window.

■ **Zoom In Vertical and Zoom Out Vertical.** These work in the same way as Zoom In and Zoom
Out, except without using the cursor as a reference and concentrating on the vertical display.

■ **Zoom In Tracks and Zoom Out Tracks.** These offer a great way to take a closer vertical look
at the selected tracks.

■ **Zoom Selected Tracks.** This works in a manner similar to Zoom In Tracks and Zoom Out
Tracks, except not only does it make the selected tracks larger, it also makes the tracks
that aren't selected smaller. This is great when you want a closer look at a track but you
still want to see the big picture.

The one thing that really sets the Zoom menu apart from other zoom tools is that it has its own
Undo and Redo section. If you make a change to your view that turns out being worse than your
previous view, you can just undo the view and revert back to your previous view. This is the only
way you can undo a zoom, because a zoom is not considered an actual edit. That is, you will not
see any zoom actions in the project history.

Macros

What if you had the option to create your own special functions that would combine multiple actions into one simple command? Choosing Macros in the Edit menu makes this possible. You can create your own commands using the File menu's Key Commands submenu. If you find yourself performing a particular action on a regular basis, I highly recommend setting up your own simple macro to make the process faster and less monotonous. I won't go into detail on how to set up a macro here, but more information is available in Appendix B, "More Shortcuts."

Even More Ways to Select Events

Moving back to the third section, which I previously skipped over, you find the Select option. This includes a list of selection commands, including the following:

- **Select All.** One of the most common selections, Select All (which you can also execute by pressing Ctrl+A) selects everything in the window or editor that's currently open.

- **Select None.** The opposite of the Select All function, Select None deselects everything that is currently selected in the open window or editor.

- **Invert.** Choose this to select everything that isn't already selected and to deselect everything that is already selected within the window or editor.

- **In Loop.** Choose this to select everything located between the left and right locators. Note: If a note or part extrudes past the left or right locator but is within the locators, it will be selected in its entirety.

- **From Start to Cursor and From Cursor to End.** Use these to select everything on either side of the cursor.

- **Equal Pitch All Octaves.** In the In-Place editor or Key editor, if you first select a note as a reference, you can use choose this command to select all the other notes that share the same pitch within the part you're working on.

- **Equal Pitch Same Octave.** If you only want to select the notes that are located in the same 12-step pitch range as the currently selected note, choose this option.

- **Select Controllers in Note Range.** If, after selecting several notes, you also want to select the controller data that went along with the notes, choose Select Controllers in Note Range. This is very much like the Auto Select Controllers function except it's more *manual* than automatic.

- **Select Event.** Like Zoom to Event, Select Event can only be used within the sample editor.

- **All on Selected Tracks.** Using this command enables you to select all the events on only the tracks you have selected.

■ **Left Selection Side to Cursor and Right Selection Side to Cursor.** When using the Range tool, if you want to snap one side of your range (i.e., the blue box) to the cursor, you can do so by using Left Selection Side to Cursor or Right Selection Side to Cursor. Simplify this step even further by pressing the E or D key on your computer keyboard to snap the left side or the right side of the box to the cursor, respectively.

There is one more way to select multiple parts or tracks that you should know about it. Say you want to select multiple parts that aren't adjacent to each other. In this scenario, drawing an object selection box or using the Range tool will not work. Instead, all you need to do is click each object you want to select with the OST while simultaneously holding down the Ctrl key on your computer keyboard. When you are finished clicking each individual part, release the Ctrl key; all the parts you clicked will remain selected. This selection method comes in very handy in a lot of cases.

8 A Closer Look at Quantizing MIDI

So far you've experienced the quantize display, the Length Q (length quantize) display, and snap on the toolbar. You stumbled upon the Quantize section of the MIDI menu. You've learned how quantize affects the Note display grid and how notes stick to the grid according to the setting in the quantize display when you use the Snap function. What you haven't learned yet is how to quantize multiple notes or the events in an entire part so that they stick to the grid. This is accomplished with a process called *quantizing*, and all quantizing is done from the Quantize section of the MIDI menu.

Using Over Quantize

The simplest way to automatically quantize multiple notes or parts is by using the Over Quantize command in the MIDI menu's Quantize section. This moves all selected notes to the nearest quantize grid location, meaning if you have your quantize display set to 1/16 notes, then selecting Over Quantize moves the selected notes to their nearest 1/16 note grid line. It's important that you have some understanding of *meter* so that you can determine exactly what your quantize settings need to be before you over-quantize. The good news is, even if you're not too knowledgeable about meter, you can undo the Over Quantize operation by choosing Undo from the Edit menu, changing your quantize setting, and trying again until it sounds the way you want.

To experiment with this, first close any song you may have open and open Song9 from the CD-ROM accompanying this book. Then do the following:

1. Select all the notes in Song9's bass part.

2. Play back the part. Notice that it isn't quantized; some notes fall slightly before or after the grid line.

3. Set the quantize display to 1/2 notes.

4. Open the MIDI menu and choose Over Quantize.

5. Play back the part and listen to how the notes play over each other, noticing that the part no longer sounds the way it was intended to sound. I deliberately had you over-quantize the part to the wrong quantize setting so that you can see how quantizing can go wrong.

6. Undo the quantize so that the part is once again the way it was originally.

7. Change your quantize display to 1/8 triplet.

8. Open the MIDI menu and once again select Over Quantize.

9. Play back the part and zoom in to examine the notes. Notice that they are positioned on the appropriate grid lines.

10. Once you understand how over-quantizing has affected the MIDI part, undo the quantize again and bring the part back to its original state.

Using Iterative Quantize and the Quantize Setup Dialog Box

You might notice that when you quantize a part, it starts to get a more robotic feel. That's because the notes fall exactly on the grid. Using the Iterative Quantize command enables you to compromise between sounding robotic and sounding human; with it, you select a percentage that indicates how close you want the notes to be to the quantize grid lines. To use the Iterative Quantize function, you first establish your quantize setting in the quantize display. Then open the MIDI menu and choose Quantize Setup; the dialog box in Figure 8.1 opens.

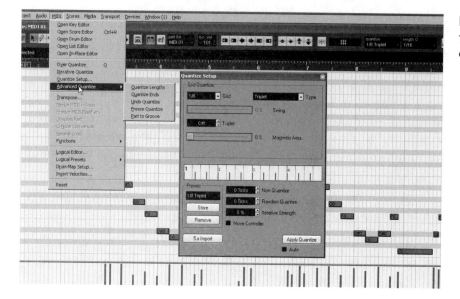

Figure 8.1

The Quantize Setup dialog box.

If you want, you can also use the Grid and Type menus to establish your basic quantize setting. To set the percentage compromise between the normal, robotic over quantize and the "human" performance, change the Iterative Strength setting to 5 percent; then close the dialog box by clicking the ✕ in the top-right corner.

Now that you have determined the strength of your compromise (5 percent), you can apply this type of quantize to the same part. Here's how:

1. Select the notes in the part.

2. Select 1/8 Triplet from the Quantize settings on the toolbar.

3. Open the MIDI menu and choose Iterative Quantize. You may notice a slight shift, but it's a subtle change.

4. Use your zoom tools to zoom in on the notes that surround measure 7. Notice how some of these notes are not on the quantize grid line. That's because the Iterative Quantize operation only moved the note 5 percent of the distance between the note and the grid line.

5. The great thing about Iterative Quantize is that you can continue to use it to move the note closer to the grid until it sounds the way you would like it to sound. With your zoom still set on the notes surrounding measure 7, again select Iterative Quantize from the MIDI menu; watch how the notes move slightly closer to the grid lines.

6. Listen and continue to move the notes closer to the grid using this method until you are satisfied with the way the performance sounds.

7. When you are finished, undo your quantize moves until you are once again back to the original unquantized part.

> **NOTE**
>
> If you open the quantize display drop-down list from the toolbar and scroll to the bottom, you'll notice a Setup heading. Selecting it is another way to open the Quantize Setup dialog box.

Swing, Tuplet, Magnetic Area, and the Grid Display

Select the notes within the part and open the Quantize Setup dialog box once again. Just below the Grid and Type display menus is the Swing percentage slider. This slider enables you to compromise the swing between a straight quantize and a triplet quantize. At 0 percent swing, the quantize will be straight; at 100 percent swing, the quantize will equal triplet. The swing slider works only when you have Straight selected from the Type menu. This can be a very useful tool in helping you find that exact swing groove you need.

Below the swing slider is a display menu called Tuplet. This enables you multiply the quantize division so that you can divide the note as far as possible if needed. It's easiest to see what's happening to the quantize in the grid display located in the middle of the Quantize Setup dialog box.

As you increase the divisions in the Tuplet display menu, you'll notice more divisions (indicated by blue lines) in the quantize grid. In a sense, it creates its own invisible grid within the visible grid. This enables you to get some very precise quantizations.

The Magnetic Area slider located just under the Tuplet display menu enables you to set a distance that notes can be from the grid before they are pulled in toward the magnetic grid line. Using this feature could prevent you from pulling a note that was intentionally off beat closer to the grid line when quantizing. The magnetic zones appear on the grid display as you adjust the slider.

Non Quantize and Random Quantize

Located just above the Iterative Strength display menu are the Non Quantize and Random Quantize display menus. The Non Quantize menu works in a similar way to how the Magnetic Area slider works; it enables you to specify how many ticks (120ths of a 1/16 note) away a note needs to be from the grid before it is quantized. The Random Quantize setting enables you to specify a maximum amount by which you'd like your note to be off beat. Then, when you quantize the notes, it randomly places the notes somewhere between the grid and your defined setting in Random Quantize. This is as "human" as a computer can get when automatically quantizing a part.

The Presets Section

The Presets section enables you to save the quantize settings you've established so that you can recall them from the quantize display on the toolbar or within the Quantize Setup dialog box. There are two very important things to remember: One is that when you store a preset using the Store button, make sure that the display box is blank. A new name will be created, and you won't be able to change it in this menu. It will not allow you to save over another saved preset. The other thing to remember is to be very careful to avoid removing the wrong preset when you click the Remove button. You can easily remove the presets that come with the program if you're not careful. Finally, if you need to import saved quantize setups from Cubase 5.0, you can do so by clicking on the 5.x Import button.

Apply Quantize, Auto, and Move Controller

When you have the setting you're happy with, you can click Apply Quantize to quantize the selected notes with your new settings. Optionally, click the Auto checkbox to apply the change to the selected parts as you make your adjustments in the dialog box. Check the Move Controller checkbox if you want the controller events to move along with the notes you have selected. (This is sort of like Auto Select Controllers on the toolbar.)

Advanced Quantize

If I had created Cubase, I'm not sure I would have called these Advanced Quantize tools because there's nothing in this section that's a whole lot more difficult than in the last section of the MIDI menu's Quantize section. Nonetheless, the tools in this section are as follows:

- **Quantize Ends.** When you have a note(s) selected, the Quantize Ends option adjusts the end point of the note(s) to the nearest grid line defined in the quantize display. This in turn affects the length of the note—although not the note's start position. The Length Q setting has no effect when you're quantizing ends, but the quantize setup settings do affect the grid lines, which in turn affect the quantizing end point.

- **Quantize Length.** The Quantize Length option works in a slightly different way from Quantize Ends. Like Quantize Ends, it does not affect the note's start point, but it uses the start point and the end point to determine the note's length and then adjusts the end point so that the note's length would fall appropriately within the grid if the note itself was on the grid. It works with the Length Q setting but can also work with the quantize setup when the Length Q setting is set to Quantize Link.

> **NOTE**
>
> Getting the Quantize Length and Quantize Ends options to work exactly as planned can be a little tricky. If you want to be precise, it may be easier in many cases to just adjust the lengths manually with the OST or the Info Line.

- **Undo Quantize.** Undo Quantize is similar to Undo Zoom because you can use it to undo only your last quantize, as opposed to undoing your last edit. Unlike Undo Zoom, though, you can also undo a quantize within the Edit menu using its Undo option.

- **Freeze Quantize.** Freeze Quantize can come in handy, especially if you have a triplet feel inside a straight feel. Using Freeze Quantize, you can first select the group of notes to which you'd like to apply a triplet feel, "freeze" the notes with the triplet feel, and then go back and select the whole part and quantize the part to a straight feel. You can also use it to freeze various other difficult groups of notes. The important thing to know is that once you freeze a quantize, you can't undo the quantize from the frozen part. Freeze Quantize is permanent.

Creating Your Own Quantize Groove

Say you have a drum or bass groove that you really like, but it doesn't fit the grid exactly. You may not want to quantize the groove, but you still want your other parts to fit the groove of the part you like so well. Creating your own quantize groove can help you take care of that little problem. Here's how:

> **NOTE**
>
> You're going to use my funky unquantized bass part in Song9 for this example, so make sure it's back to its original state.

1. First, close the Key editor.

2. In the project window, use the Split tool to split the bass part at measures 3 and 7.

3. Double-click the part you just created between measures 3 and 7 to open it in the Key editor.

4. From the MIDI menu's Quantize section, under Advanced Quantize, select Part to Groove. Notice how the grid lines move to the start positions of the notes within the part.

5. Open the menu on the toolbar's quantize display and notice how there is a new quantize called "MIDI 01 Tempo 120.00 Signature 4/4 4 bars." This is your new quantize groove.

6. Choose Setup at the bottom the toolbar's quantize display menu. The quantize groove you just created is displayed in the grid display. Notice that there are two new drop-down menus with your created groove: Pre Quantize and Max Move. The new quantize groove is also now stored as a preset in the preset section, and there is an Orig. Position checkbox.

7. Set the Pre Quantize to 16T and the Max Move to 8T in the Quantize Setup dialog box (more info on these options in a moment).

8. Close the Key editor.

9. Double-click between measures 7 and 11 on the bass part in the project window to open the second half of the bass part in the Key editor.

10. Select all the notes within the bass part.

11. Open the Quantize Setup dialog box and click Apply Quantize. The notes move to the groove grid you created with the first half of the bass part.

After you've created a quantize groove, you can use it as many times and wherever you want within Cubase by pulling it up from the menu. You can use it with Over Quantize and Iterative Quantize as well as applying it from within the Quantize Setup dialog box.

Using the Pre Quantize enables you to quantize the part before you apply the groove quantize, which usually helps get the notes closer to their groove destination. The Max Move option is similar to setting the magnetic area of a note. By setting a magnetic area, you're specifying the maximum distance the quantize can move a note to get to the grid line. This helps eliminate the possibility of moving off notes you don't want to move. You can use the up and down arrows on the side of the display to scroll through the familiar settings (such as 8th, 8T, 16th, 32nd, and so on), or you can click the display to reveal a slider that enables you to adjust the setting in ticks as opposed to note values.

Checking the Orig. Position checkbox causes the selected part to revert to its original position on the grid when you use Apply Quantize. This can be useful in helping you determine the proper Pre Quantize and Max Move values. A lot of times, you have to play around with these settings to get the desired result; the Orig. Position ensures that you can get back to your starting point without having to continuously undo your settings.

Another great thing about creating your own quantize groove is that you can also use an audio file to create a MIDI groove. This involves setting up what's called *hit points* on an audio loop and then using those hit points to create a groove quantize map such as the one you just created with a MIDI part. For more information, see page 225 of the Cubase 4 manual.

9 Working with MIDI Effects and Modifiers

Back in Chapter 6, "Working with MIDI in the Project Window," you explored the inspector in the project window, including a bit about MIDI modifiers and MIDI effects sends and inserts. As promised, I'm now going to walk you through all these useful MIDI tools. MIDI modifiers and effects both work in a similar way, processing MIDI data in real time. That means that by using either of these tools, you can dramatically change the sound of your MIDI part without altering the actual MIDI part itself.

Before you begin, close any songs you have open and open Song10 from the CD-ROM accompanying this book. Play the song from start to end; as you'll see, this is the song you've been working with except it's been altered with a few simple edits and with a lot of MIDI effects and modifiers. You probably think some of the changes sound strange, but I can't be blamed for all of them; Cubase has randomly written some of the music. (Of course, I'll take credit for anything you like.)

Using the MIDI Modifiers

Each track in Cubase has its own set of MIDI modifiers, all of which are found in the inspector. If it's not already open, launch the inspector and select the Triangle MIDI track, making sure the MIDI Modifiers tab is selected in the inspector, as shown in Figure 9.1.

> **NOTE**
>
> As mentioned in Chapter 6, you should make sure that the checkboxes in the Display Setup dialog box that relate to MIDI modifiers, MIDI inserts, and MIDI sends are checked. That way, you'll be able to view their tabs within the inspector.

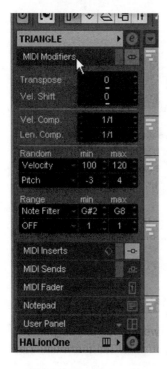

Figure 9.1
The MIDI Modifiers tab.

The MIDI Modifiers tab contains the following controls:

■ Transpose and Velocity Shift

■ Velocity Compression

■ Length Compression

■ Random effect modifiers

■ Range filters and limiters

Transpose and Velocity Shift

The Transpose and Velocity Shift sliders at the top of the MIDI Modifiers tab are similar to the Transpose and Velocity tools in the Info Line, above the part display in the project window. When you use the Transpose and Velocity tools in the Info Line, only the part is affected; when using the similar controls in the MIDI Modifiers tab, the settings for the entire MIDI track are affected. Also, when you use the Pitch Transpose and Velocity Shift within the Info Line, the notes and velocities change to their new settings within the note display. Using the controls in the MIDI Modifier has the same audible effect, but the notes remain in place within the Note display.

Velocity Compression

The MIDI Modifiers tab's Velocity Compression tool is very similar to the Compress/Expand option in the Velocity editor accessible from the MIDI menu's Functions area. One subtle difference is that instead of working with percentages, the MIDI Modifiers tab's Velocity Compression tool works with fractions. I'm no math wizard, but even I know that fractions and percentages are just different ways of saying the same thing. The only other real difference is that using the setting in the MIDI menu actually changes the velocity for the part or whatever notes you've selected, whereas the MIDI Modifiers tab's Velocity Compression tool only affects the track without actually changing the velocity values.

Length Compression

A new feature, Length Compression, alters the length of each individual note on the MIDI track according to your setting. For instance, a setting of 1/2 cuts the length of each note on the track in half, and a setting of 2/1 doubles the length of every note on the track. If you examine the bass track within the inspector, you will notice that the Length Compression has been changed to 1/2, which in turn has shortened every note on its track during playback without affecting the actual length of the notes on the track.

Random Effect Modifiers

Whenever you see the word *random* in Cubase, it means the computer is writing the part. The MIDI Modifiers tab includes four variables that you can instruct the computer to affect randomly:

- **Pitch.** When you choose Pitch, the computer randomly changes the pitch of each note by randomly shifting the pitch values up or down by as many as 120 semitones.

- **Velocity.** When you choose Velocity, the computer randomly changes the velocity setting of each note up or down 120 steps.

- **Position.** When you choose Position, the computer randomly moves each note forward or backward in time up to 500 ticks in each direction on the timeline.

- **Length.** When you choose the Length setting, the computer randomly lengthens or shortens each note by as many as 500 ticks.

You can use as many as two random effect modifiers on each track at one time. For a demo of the Pitch and Velocity random settings, see the Triangle track; notice how the triangle turns into several different instruments. That's because the patch in the Hip Hop Kit from the Halion One Sample player has a different sample for every key. The random velocity might not stand out quite as much, but it adds some random dynamics to the part.

The Length and Position random settings are used on the Funk Guitar track. (There is also an echo effect on the track, which I'll get to in a little bit.) The notes shift randomly out of time, and the length of each note is affected at random. Like the other modifiers, these random modifiers do not change the way the notes, lengths, locations, or velocities are displayed on the grid.

> **NOTE**
>
> The tricky thing about using random settings is that they hardly ever sound the same way twice. If you want to turn a random setting into a fixed part, you can do so in one of two ways: by freezing the MIDI modifiers and by creating an audio file of the part. I explain how to freeze a MIDI modifier at the end of this chapter; you'll learn how to export a MIDI part as an audio part in Chapter 13, "Now That You Know Everything There Is to Know about Editing MIDI in Cubase . . ."

Range Filters and Limiters

Cubase offers two range filters and limiter settings, with as many as four options each:

- **Velocity limiter.** The velocity limiter works similarly to a compressor/limiter. It enables you to establish a high and a low velocity setting, with any velocity that falls outside that range being pulled into the range you've defined, thus eliminating the possibilities of a note being played too soft or too loud. Any note that has a velocity higher than the high velocity setting will be lowered to the high velocity setting, and any note that has a velocity lower than the low velocity setting will be raised to the low velocity setting. The notes with velocities within the range settings will not be affected. For a closer examination of this modifier, check out the bass track in Song10; its velocity limiter song has been adjusted so that no velocity is lower than 90. In playback, you should notice that the bass sounds as if it has been played harder than it was originally played.

- **Velocity filter.** The velocity filter operates in the exact opposite way. Every note that contains a velocity between the velocity filter's high and low settings is silenced; only the notes outside the filter's velocity range are played back at their original velocity setting. This is great for getting rid of the ghost notes I mentioned earlier in the book.

- **Note limiter.** When the note limiter is used, notes that fall outside of the defined pitch range are played within the limited range's octave instead of in its original octave. (Note that if you set your limits to less than a one-octave range, things get a little strange. The notes that have no place to go within the octave default to playing the middle note of your defined range. For example, if you narrow your range to A1 to C1, and the note in the part is a G2, the G2 will play as a B1. This can create a completely different harmonic structure to your song, so be careful when setting the range.

- **Note filter.** When the note filter is set, all notes that fall outside the defined range are silenced. Again, this modifier has no visual effect on the displayed notes or velocities.

NOTE

If you've been keeping an eye on your performance meter, you may have noticed that it's a little more active than it was before. That's because the effects and modifiers are actually processing the MIDI events in real time, which creates a heavier load on your computer's CPU. If you play back the track and hear pops and crackles, try adjusting your latency settings within the control panel of your sound card. I currently have my latency set at 1,024 samples, which isn't the best for live monitoring, but you probably won't notice any difference while going over these exercises. You can even go higher than 1,024 samples if you're still hearing crackles and digital noise bursts.

Using the MIDI Effects

Using a MIDI effect as another alternative to changing the sound of your MIDI track can offer even more creative possibilities. There are two possible ways to use a MIDI effect: One is through what's called a *MIDI insert*, and the other is through what's called a MIDI send. Both of these tabs should be visible from the inspector on the left side of the project window.

Inserts versus Send Effects

The Inserts and Sends sections of the inspector use the same MIDI effects, but they operate in slightly different ways. When you use a MIDI effect in an insert, it processes only the track in which that particular insert is active. MIDI send effects work with individual tracks the same way a MIDI insert works, but they also give you the option of sending the processed MIDI data to another MIDI channel and output. This means, for instance, using Song10 as a reference, that you can delay the Funk Guitar track but play back the effect of the delay on the electric piano as well as the funk guitar so that the electric piano echoes the funk guitar. There is also a pre/post fader switch button on each send that enables you to specify whether you want the effect on the pre track (that is, the unaffected MIDI track) or the post track (as it's heard after the MIDI modifiers and inserts have taken effect). For an example of this in Song10, take a closer look at the Shamisen sends by selecting the MIDI Sends tab in the inspector while the Shamisen track is selected. Notice that the output of the MIDI echo effect is being sent to 8-Halion One, which is the Old Tape Strings track.

To select a MIDI effect on either a send or an insert, simply click an empty effect window; a drop-down list appears, with 16 different MIDI effects (see Figure 9.2). If a track is selected, and if that track is actively using an effect as either a send or an insert, the effect indicator on its tab will appear blue. To disable the effect on the selected track, simply click the box to the left of the blue indicator on either the MIDI Sends or MIDI Inserts tab (the box will turn yellow when the effects are disabled). Disabling effects in this way can be useful when you're trying to distinguish the result of the effect on a track.

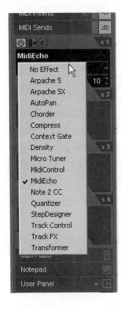

Figure 9.2

Selecting a MIDI effect.

When an effect is loaded as either a send or an insert, you can edit its settings by clicking on the e button located just to the right of the effect's on button (just to the right of the pre/post fader button on the effect send). Figure 9.3 shows the MIDI Sends section, highlighting all the controls I've mentioned so far.

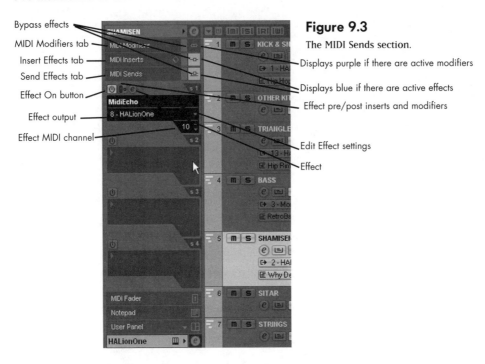

Figure 9.3

The MIDI Sends section.

The MIDI Plug-ins

I won't go over all the MIDI plug-ins in detail, but I want to give you a taste of what each of them is capable of doing by using examples in Songio. If you'd like to learn more about each particular effect, open the Help menu, choose Documentation (Adobe Acrobat), and select Plug-in Reference.

> **NOTE**
>
> To get a better understanding of how each effect is performing in Songio, it may be a good idea to try soloing a track that I'm referring to by selecting the solo button on the appropriate track. Using this method will enable you to concentrate on how a particular effect is changing the sound of the individual track I'm referring to.

- **Arpache 5** and **Arpache SX.** Both of these MIDI effects are arpeggiators. They work best on sustained chords and play each individual note of the chord in an up-and-down pattern or in a pattern that you create yourself. You can adjust the speed and the length of each note as it's played from the controls within. I've used the Arpache SX to create a slow arpeggio from the chords that are held out on the Strings track. Take a close look and listen to the Strings track because the notes you are hearing are not programmed in; they are being played by the Arpache SX.

- **Autopan.** Instead of programming your pan in a controller lane, you can use this effect to automatically pan the MIDI instrument in a variety of ways and speeds. I used the Autopan as an insert effect on the acoustic guitar so that it would pan back and forth between the left and right speakers.

- **Chorder.** The Chorder takes a single-note melody and transforms each note into a harmonic chord. You can use preset chords or create your own chords for it to play. The Chorder was one of several effects I used on the Shamisen track, which was originally just a single note part. (I also changed the sound in Halion One because a chord on a Shamisen doesn't sound very nice.)

- **Compress.** This effect isn't a lot different from most of the other types of MIDI compression you've used so far. This particular plug-in more closely resembles an audio compressor. I used this as an insert on the Bass track to keep the velocities more consistent and to make the bass seem a little louder and less dynamic.

- **Context Gate.** This MIDI effect enables you to silence wrong notes from chords or multiple notes from a mono part, or it can be used in a similar way as the note range limiter modifier to remove notes you don't want to be played. There is no example of this effect within Songio.

- **Note to CC.** This effect creates a continuous controller event for every note that's played. I used this to create a panning effect in the Triangle part that pans when a different note is played.

- **Quantizer.** This effect applies real-time quantization to the notes without actually quantizing them. This can be great for swinging a part without having to actually move the notes within the Note display. I used the quantizer on the Electric Piano part so that it would create note clusters out of the little lick at the end of the part.

- **Step Designer.** This is used to create a pattern in step mode (similar to old hardware sequencers and drum machines) and loop the pattern according to what note is played. You can create a different pattern for every note. I used this to create the new Sitar pattern on one note. I also sequenced a blank pattern and assigned it to a note number so that I could turn the pattern on and off during the sequence.

- **Density.** This is another random effect. At a 100 percent setting, there is no effect. At settings of less than 100 percent, notes are randomly muted; at settings over 100 percent, notes are randomly added. I used this effect to randomly add some notes to the Ac Guitar track.

- **Microtuner.** This can be used to make fine-tune adjustments according to each pitch in the scale. This is great for instruments that are normally tuned in a way other than standard chromatic tuning. I used it to make the electric piano sound a little out of tune.

- **MIDI Control.** This was designed to be a control panel for use with synths so that you could control their parameters remotely. You still have to change the settings of the parameters yourself, and there's not a lot of automatic processing involved. I did not use this plug-in in Songio.

- **MIDI Echo.** Unlike an audio delay, this effect plays another note(s) according to your settings. I used this on the Funk Guitar track.

- **Track Control.** This is another control that is similar to the MIDI control, but it is set up to control some synths that are compatible with the GS and XG standards. The Monologue synth is compatible, so I used it to tweak the bass sound. I didn't record any automation with these controls, but keep in mind that you can use the power of automation to create some really interesting textures when using a tool with controls.

- **Track FX.** This is very similar to the tools that are automatically located on each track. The only real difference is a handy-dandy Scale Transpose tool, which works similarly to the Transpose tool when quantizing pitches according to a scale. There is no example of this in the demo song.

- **Transformer.** Not to be confused with a semi-trailer that can turn into a robot, this is a complex processor that enables you to create many formulas where you can automate a complicated process. In this song, I simply used a preset formula to convert velocities to MIDI volume on the Other Kit track.

Turning a MIDI Effect into an Editable MIDI Part

When you have the MIDI effect you've been looking for, there are many directions you can go. The easiest, of course, would be to leave things the way they are. If you would like to free your processor from the burden of all the real-time processing, you could bounce the track down as an audio file, or you could freeze the MIDI modifiers and bounce down the effects to a MIDI part.

When you explored the MIDI menu, you skipped the Freeze MIDI Modifiers function. Now that you are familiar with MIDI effects and modifiers, the only foreign word in that function's name is *freeze*. When you freeze a MIDI modifier, you transform the current MIDI track into a processed track. When you freeze a track, the settings in your MIDI modifier are bypassed, and the MIDI track repositions the notes on the Note display so that they reflect what you were previously hearing. If everything goes according to plan, there should be no audible difference between a frozen track and an unfrozen track. When you have frozen your modifiers (and, just so you know, this means all MIDI insert effects and modifiers for the selected track), you free your CPU from all that real-time processing, and you create a new part that you can edit just as you would have edited the original part. The fact that you can now edit affected parts reveals a whole new direction you can take with your music.

NOTE

The problem with freezing a track is you completely lose your original recording. If you're like me, this might freak you out because you may want to go back to the original part to make changes to it someday. But don't panic—you can work around this by duplicating the entire track *before* you freeze. Once you have a duplicate track, you can *mute* the duplicate track so that you never have to hear it with the mix, but it will always be there in case you change your mind later.

Freezing a part is very simple. Just select the track you'd like to freeze and then select Freeze MIDI Modifiers from the MIDI menu. *Voilà!* It's like magic. Practice by duplicating and freezing a track that is going to look completely different after it has been frozen:

1. Select the Sitar track.

2. From the Project menu, select Duplicate Track. A duplicate of the Sitar track, called Copy of Sitar, is created and placed underneath the original.

3. Mute the Copy of Sitar track by clicking the track's Mute button.

4. Select the Sitar track once again.

5. Open the MIDI menu and choose Freeze MIDI Modifiers.

6. Open the In-Place editor for both the new (frozen) Sitar track and the Copy of Sitar track. You should see that the events within each part are completely different and that the new (frozen) Sitar track's effects are currently deactivated under the MIDI Insert tab (see Figure 9.4).

Effects are deactivated after
Freeze MIDI Modifiers is selected

After applying the Freeze
MIDI Modifiers command

Before applying the Freeze
MIDI Modifiers command

Figure 9.4

The frozen Sitar track compared to the unfrozen Sitar track. Notice how the new track appears as it sounds, and the old track appears as it did before Freeze MIDI Modifiers was selected.

NOTE

A send effect cannot be frozen like an insert effect because the output is usually another track. The only remedy for this problem I could find was exporting the send as an audio file by capturing the output of the synth's audio. Even this is a little tricky, however. Perhaps someone from team Steinberg will come up with a nice solution to this little oversight someday.

Merge MIDI in Loop and Dissolving Parts

I want to take a moment to discuss the Merge MIDI in Loop function, just underneath the Freeze MIDI Modifiers function in the MIDI menu. You use this function to combine all your MIDI tracks into one track. This can only be achieved while working in the project window. When you select Merge MIDI in Loop, a prompt appears, asking if you'd like to include the inserts and sends as well as erase the destination and include chase.

Although this sounds like a nifty way to clean up your project window, you should be aware that this is intended for advanced users. When you merge tracks, your instrument and MIDI channel settings get merged along with them. I recommend that you don't mess with this unless all your tracks are played using the same multi-timbral synth or sampler, just so you can avoid confusion. Once tracks have been merged, you can unmerge them using the Dissolve Part function, also in the MIDI menu; that said, some information that is lost during a merge will not be available after the part has been dissolved (unmerged). For more information, refer to pages 292–294 of the Cubase manual.

10 The Drum Editor

You've probably noticed that drum parts don't really follow the pitch grid like a bass part or a keyboard part would. That's because it would be unusual for a drum kit to be tuned like a piano or a guitar. Even though drums do have a pitch and can be tuned, you wouldn't normally tune a drum or percussion kit to a chromatic scale.

When you're dealing with drum kits, you have to stop thinking about pitch and start thinking about MIDI note numbers. Remember in Chapter 9, "Working with MIDI Effects and Modifiers," when the computer rewrote the Triangle part in Song10, using the random Pitch MIDI modifier to change it into a multiple percussion part? It didn't alter pitch; it altered MIDI note numbers. Another difference between a note played on a chromatic instrument (such as a guitar) and a drum is that *holding* a note on a drum doesn't sound much different from playing a staccato note on a drum. Note lengths almost become a moot point, especially when you're dealing with a MIDI drum part.

These two differences—the use of note numbers rather than pitch, and the demotion of note length in importance—are reasons why Cubase decided to incorporate a special editor for drum parts: the Drum editor. Although there's no reason you couldn't edit drum parts within the Key editor or project window, the Drum editor makes the whole process easier.

To get the hang of using the Drum editor, close any songs you might have open in Cubase and open Song11 from the CD-ROM accompanying this book. The song opens with the drum kit part on track 1 displayed in the Drum editor. Notice how, on the left side of the screen, you no longer have a keyboard; instead, you have a list of drums, cymbals, and various percussion instruments alongside note numbers (such as C1, D2, F#4, and so on). Notice, too, how the Note display now has little diamond shapes as opposed to different-sized boxes to represent notes with no reference to length. As you can see, using the diamonds instead of the boxes in the Note display makes the Note display much easier to read and edit drum parts. By default, two controller lanes appear at the bottom of the screen, even if there aren't two lanes of controller events to display. You can alter the display of these controller lanes as well as edit the controller lane events in the Drum editor in the exact same way as in the Key editor. (Since you already learned how to work with controller lanes in Chapter 4, "The Controller Lanes and the Line Tool," go ahead and close one of the two controller lanes so you can get a better look at the Note display.)

> **NOTE**
>
> To open the Drum editor in any part, first select the part and then select Open Drum Editor from the MIDI menu.

Toolbar Overview

Not surprisingly, the Drum editor's toolbar is a bit different from the Key editor's and project window's. For example, the Drum editor's toolbar lacks a Pencil tool, Split tool, and Glue tool; likewise, the Line tool button's Paint tool option is missing, as is the Length Q setting. At the same time, the Drum editor contains tools not found elsewhere—although some of the Drum editor's tools do match up with tools you've explored already. Here's a rundown of the available tools with which you are likely unfamiliar:

- **Drumstick tool.** The Drumstick tool is used like the Pencil tool to create notes, but if you click on a pre-existing note with the Drumstick tool, the note will be erased.

- **Insert Length.** Instead of having a Length Q setting, the Drum editor contains an Insert Length setting, which establishes the default length of any notes you create.

- **Global Quantize.** Located next to the Snap Function button is the Global Quantize button. Unlike the Key editor, the Drum editor enables you to set different quantize values for each individual drum (note number). It may seem backward, but Global Quantize works like Quantize in the Key editor. When Global Quantize is active, every note moves according to the setting in the quantize display. When Global Quantize is not active, the notes are quantized by the setting in the Quantize column to the right of the Instrument column and to the left of the Note display (depending on your view, you may have to pull the Note display to the right to expose the Quantize column underneath).

> **NOTE**
>
> You may have noticed that instead of revealing note numbers in its display, the mouse pointer displays the drum sound over which your pointer is positioned. The columns just left of the Note display reveal the drum sound list and the settings of each individual sound (by note number). The number of columns can vary slightly, depending on the type of drum map you're using. (You will experiment with drum maps a little later in this chapter.) For now, you should see a column for pitch (note number), instrument, and quantize, and a narrow empty column just to the left of the Pitch column.

- **OST.** If you want to hear the drum sounds in the drum kit, you can do so by using the OST to select the empty box in the column just to the left of the Pitch column. This is similar to using the OST on the Key editor's keyboard. If you want to hear a particular note, select the Audio Feedback button and click it with the OST just as you would within the Key editor.

- **Solo Editor.** This button enables you to mute the rest of the tracks in the project menu and concentrate on the part(s) within the Drum editor during playback.

- **Solo Instrument.** When active and using a drum map, the Solo Instrument button (located just to the right of the Solo Editor button) enables you to solo a particular instrument in the drum track by selecting the instrument you'd like to hear from the Instrument column. When using a drum name list, the Solo Instrument button has no use.

NOTE

I will be discussing drum maps and drum name lists a little later in this chapter.

Creating and Editing Drum Parts

For the most part, creating and editing drum parts is handled in the same way you handle notes in the Key editor. There are, however, a few minor but important differences

One is that when you are working with the Info Line's Length parameter, you can alter the length value in the Drum editor, but because the Drum editor's Note display does not represent note lengths, you will not be able to see the actual length changes in the Drum editor. For this reason, I highly recommend you avoid changing note lengths with the Info Line in the Drum editor but instead use the Key editor to change the note lengths. Even though drum sounds are usually "one shot" samples, if notes overlap or are doubled, there is usually an adverse effect. It's important to know your note lengths are not overlapping.

Another is that when you create a note with the Drumstick tool, the note will be positioned according to your Snap and Quantize settings. That means if Global Quantize is active, Snap is activated, and your quantize display is set to 1/4 notes, the note will be positioned on the nearest 1/4 grid line and will *not* take the instrument's individual Quantize setting into account. If Snap is activated and Global Quantize is deactivated, the note will be positioned on the grid according to the instrument's Quantize setting. If the Snap is not activated, the note will be positioned wherever you click. The Drum editor's Snap types are exactly the same as the Snap types within the Key editor. When a note is created with the Drumstick tool, the velocity will become whatever the insert velocity display is set to. If you're moving multiple notes from different instruments and Snap is on but Global Quantize is off, each of the notes will snap to the Quantize setting of each individual instrument.

> **NOTE**
>
> Just because this editor is called the Drum editor doesn't mean that you are strictly limited to editing drum parts in it. You can open *any* MIDI track in the Drum editor. This may seem a little silly, but sometimes, when you need to focus on individual note numbers (pitches) of other instruments, the Drum editor is the best tool for the job. The important thing is that you understand how each editor works and keep an open mind so you can decide which editor will work best for the edit you'd like to make.

> **NOTE**
>
> Working with multiple MIDI parts is also possible within the Drum editor. For more information on working with several parts at once, see Appendix A, "Working with Multiple MIDI Tracks in an Editor."

Working with Drum Maps

The single most important aspect of the Drum editor is its ability to work with drum maps. A *drum map* determines which drum sound is playing on what note number, as well as how the notes will be displayed in the Drum editor's Note display.

Drum maps were created because MIDI instrument manufacturers were setting up drum kits on their instruments with no regard to how their note numbers related to the note numbers used in other manufacturers' drum kits. That is, the note numbers were not standardized. This made things difficult for the programmers like you and me when it came to experimenting with various instruments and drum sounds for songs.

For example, you might record a song with your Yamaha drum machine but later decide that the sounds on your Roland drum machine were more dope. But when you switched instruments, you'd find that the kick part was playing on the Roland's crash cymbal, and the snare part was playing on the Roland's cowbell. Of course, this would sound like garbage, so you'd begrudgingly go back to using your Yamaha drum machine that you didn't really like because at least it *worked*.

In time, manufacturers got together and came up with General MIDI to control default instrument settings, so that switching from, say, one synth to another would not be a big issue with prerecorded parts. General MIDI brought MIDI to the next level, defining the note number on which each of the default drum kits instruments would fall as well as which instruments were active on each of the 16 MIDI channels. (General MIDI is also the reason a MIDI file will sound one way when played on your cell phone and another way when played on your computer, but with the same musical arrangement—that is, it doesn't play a harpsichord sound when it should be playing a marimba.)

With the advent of General MIDI, *some* people's headaches went away—although General MIDI didn't put an end to drum kit–setup problems. For example, although it allowed for some standardization with regard to note numbers, it didn't enable you to customize the drum-kit setup. Everyone wants their setup to be as easy and efficient as possible, but what's "easy and efficient" isn't the same for everyone. Setting up your own drum map as opposed to working with a General MIDI drum map can help you work with drum sounds the way you feel most comfortable and productive. Even though it takes time to set up a drum map, like naming a track, it will save you time when you decide to make changes later on.

The way the drum sounds are currently listed on the left side of your screen is the default General MIDI name list. The drum kit that you're actually hearing is the Hip Hop Kit 2 preset from the Halion One sample player VST instrument included with Cubase. If you are familiar with drum instruments and sounds, you may find as you listen to the sounds listed in the General MIDI name list that some things don't quite add up.

> **NOTE**
>
> A drum map is a more advanced version of a name list. I won't go into detail on how to create a name list; if you know and understand drum maps, there's no point in learning the name list. On each controller lane is a small menu for the currently loaded drum maps and for the currently loaded name lists. When using drum maps, you will only need to use the Drum Maps menu.

If you use the OST to select the empty box in the column to the left of the instrument name at the top of the list, you will probably think that the names somewhat resemble the sounds you are hearing. You'll find that Long Whistle, however, doesn't sound anything like a whistle. Instead, it sounds something like a sci-fi Martian's phaser ray gun. If you really want the sound of a whistle, you won't find it in this hip-hop kit. The Halion One's programmer has taken a few liberties replacing certain General MIDI instruments with what he felt necessary to make the proper Hip Hop Kit 2 preset.

> **NOTE**
>
> It would make sense if Cubase came with automatically created drum maps for all the drum kits that come with the program, but unfortunately this is not the case. That said, there are some drum maps for some other popular external synths and samplers, which you can find in your program folder or on your Cubase 4 DVD.

Editing and Creating a Drum Map

When you create a drum map, you create a translation program that works between the notes you have recorded (or are playing with a MIDI instrument) and the sounds in your synth or sampler. To begin creating a drum map, you must first open the Drum Map Setup dialog box (see Figure

10.1), accessible from the MIDI menu. You can also open the Drum Map Setup dialog box by select-ing it from the drop-down menu found on a controller lane. You can resize the Drum Map Setup dialog box by dragging the bottom-right corner of the box, just as you would a window.

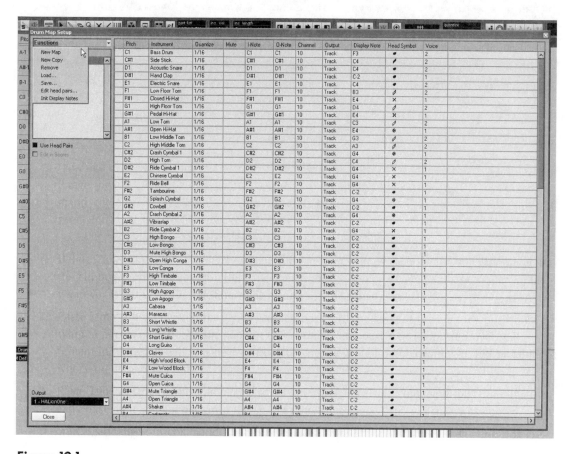

Figure 10.1

The Drum Map Setup dialog box with its Functions menu open.

The Drum Map Setup dialog box contains the following columns:

■ **Audition.** This column appears as an empty column to the left of the Pitch column. Select within this column to hear the way the instrument and note number on the corresponding row will sound.

■ **Pitch.** This represents the note number of the drum kit.

■ **Instrument.** This is simply a name for the drum sound you should be hearing on the corre-sponding note number. The name can be edited by clicking and typing.

- **Quantize.** This enables you to set up individual quantize values for each of your drum sounds.

- **"M".** The "M" stands for *mute* and offers another way to mute an instrument. This mute works differently from muting a note or part in that it actually stops any sound from happening, even when that particular key is pressed on a MIDI controller. It acts as if a filter is on a particular note and keeps the note from playing.

- **I-note.** The I-note represents the note that enters into the drum map (the input note). Changing the I-note affects how the MIDI information is recorded in Cubase. When the I-note is played on a MIDI instrument, it triggers the note number that is located in the Pitch column. This is to be used primarily when you need to set a MIDI controller to play particular note numbers instead of the note numbers it plays by default. If you already have a recorded MIDI part, such as the demo song, changing the I-note will have no effect. Two notes cannot share the same I-note, so another I-note will change to a free I-note setting when you've altered the I-note to one that already exists in the drum map.

- **O-note.** The O-note represents the note that exits the drum map (the output note). Changing the O-note affects how recorded notes are played in Cubase. For example, this enables you to take a note that appears as a C1 in the Note display and output it so that it plays as G2. When you're working with prerecorded parts, this is a way to sort of reset the instrument so that the correct sound plays on the recorded pitch (note number). Like the I-note, there can only be one O-note setting per note number.

- **Channel.** This enables you to reassign a new MIDI channel to a particular instrument. Even though it defaults on MIDI channel 10, the instruments will still play on their recorded MIDI channel unless the number is altered from its original setting.

- **Output.** This enables you to reassign a new instrument output channel. If the drum sound you're looking for is on another instrument, you can change it so that it plays back on the correct instrument here.

- **Display Note.** This setting's only purpose is to show where the note will be displayed in *score* form. This is a handy tool to make sure your drum part is readable when you need to print a drum score from the Score editor.

- **Head Symbol.** This is another scoring feature, which determines what the note will look like on the score.

- **Voice.** This enables you to set the polyphony of that one particular drum sound. You can set the polyphony from one to eight voices.

After you have set up a drum map and used the drum map within the Drum editor, the four columns that were originally displayed with the General MIDI name list will expand as a drum map to also include the M, I-note, O-note, Channel, and Output columns. When these columns are available in the Drum editor's window, you can make changes to them and resave them in the Drum editor when you save the project. Any new drum maps you create will appear in the controller lane's drop-down menu for easy access.

> **NOTE**
>
> You can alter the position of these columns by dragging them and dropping them in another location. I did notice, however, that moving the columns within the Drum editor itself was a little more unstable and harder to work with—presumably a bug in the program.

The drum map setup also has its own drop-down Functions menu in the top-left side of the window. Clicking anywhere within the Function field will open the menu of seven functions, which are described in the following list.

- **New Map.** This sets up a blank template, enabling you to create a drum map from scratch.
- **New Copy.** Choose this to create a new drum map based on a copy of a pre-existing one. It's a good alternative to starting from scratch. You just need to save the copy with your modifications.
- **Remove.** Choose this to delete the drum maps you have saved within the song. But be careful—there's no undo!
- **Load.** This enables you to import drum maps you have saved in a location other than the current song.
- **Save.** This enables you to save the drum map to a location outside the song.
- **Edit Head Pairs.** This is a scoring feature for setting up and displaying drum notes.
- **Init Display Notes.** Using this function resets all the pitches so that they are once again in sequential order. Unlike using New Map, the other settings will remain.

You can shift the instrument rows up or down within the drum map to customize your view. To do so, select the instrument row with the OST within the Pitch column and click and drag upward or downward in the drum map; a green guide line appears, showing the position of the moved row. When you release the mouse button, the row will appear between the rows where the green guide line was located. This only changes the display of the notes for easier editing; it does *not* affect the position of the note in any way as it relates to the keyboard or note number.

> **NOTE**
>
> If you want to be able to audition samples within the Drum Map Setup dialog box, you need to set the Output menu that's located in the bottom-left area of the dialog box to the instrument for which you are setting up sounds.

Loading a Drum Map

To demonstrate what a drum map can do for a drum part, I have created a drum map for you to load into the Drum editor. First, however, take a good look at the drum part in the Drum editor, scrolling all the way up and down through the note numbers. You should see some notes that are distanced from another group of notes located toward the top of the Note display. Then do the following:

1. From the controller lane's Drum Map drop-down menu, select Drum Map Setup.

2. The Drum Map Setup dialog box opens. Open the Functions menu and select Load.

3. With the CD-ROM accompanying this book loaded in your CD-ROM drive, locate the contents of the CD-ROM from the Load dialog box. (This is much like loading a song.)

4. Open the Drum Maps folder.

5. Locate, select, and load the Hip Hop drum map file.

6. Close the Drum Map Setup dialog box.

7. Open the Drum Maps menu on the controller lane and select Hip Hop. The drum map changes to reveal what's shown in Figure 10.2.

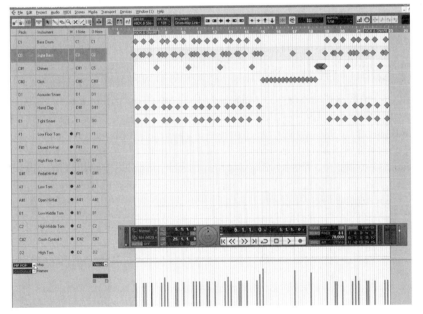

Figure 10.2

The Hip Hop drum map in action.

I'm sure you can already *see* a difference, but you will also *hear* a difference after playing the part. You can also compare the difference by alternating between the Hip Hop drum map and the default GM Drum Map, which was what was originally there. Here's a list of the changes:

■ I repositioned and renamed a drum part, which I called SUPA BASS, that once had no name and was located toward the bottom of the Note display. Now it's next to the other kick-drum part at the top of the Note display for easier viewing.

■ I renamed the drum part that was originally underneath (the SUPA BASS part) to "Click" and moved it to a new position amongst the other parts for easier viewing and editing.

■ I changed the O-note of what used to be called a side stick so that it played the wind chimes sound on note C5 instead and then renamed the instrument to "Chimes."

■ I decided that I wanted to change the snare sound at E1 to a different type of snare, so I changed the instrument output to HIP RIM KIT2 and changed the O-note to a sound I liked that was located at G0. The sound had no name, so I called it "Tight Snare."

■ Just for good measure, I changed all the MIDI channels on the sounds I was using to MIDI channel 1 and muted the sounds located above F1 so that they couldn't be used.

As you can see, a drum map can come in pretty handy when you'd like to make a few changes to the drum sounds. You can also make some of these changes by actually moving the notes to new note numbers in the Note display, but setting up drum maps give you a few more options and enables you to quickly change your setup if you want to try multiple changes.

O-Note Conversion

There's one more drum-map feature you should be aware of: O-note conversion. This function, found toward the bottom of the MIDI menu, changes notes that have been routed to different output positions (that is, notes with modified O-note values) to their position within the Note display so that they are no longer routed to the O-note but are positioned at the O-note. You consider using this function because it's possible that, in the process of routing a note with the O-note translator, there could be a micro-millisecond delay that you don't want on your drum track. Alternatively, you might just want to change the position of the notes on the Note display for better or different viewing purposes. Whatever your purpose for bypassing the O-note process, this is the function to take care of it.

> **NOTE**
>
> When doing an O-note conversion, if you have previously muted the O-note note number, the notes will become muted. This can be remedied by unmuting those particular sounds. Another important point is that for some reason (this may be a bug), the output defaults to the Track setting, which is the current track's instrument setting. If you've routed the output to another instrument, you'll have to once again re-route it to the instrument of your choice.

11 The List Editor, Logical Editor, and Project Browser

Now that you've explored the Key editor, the In-Place editor, the project window, and the Drum editor, I'm going to introduce you to a couple of other editors: the List editor and the Logical editor. I consider both of these editors to be more for advanced Cubase users. I also want to introduce you to the Project browser. You probably won't use these tools a lot, but you'll be glad you know your way around them when you need them.

The List Editor

The List editor displays MIDI information in a very detailed and numerical way. You might consider using this editor when you need to fine-tune your MIDI part in a way you can't with Cubase's other editors. To explore the List editor, begin by closing any songs you have open and opening Song12 from the CD-ROM that accompanies this book.

When the song loads, you should see a screen that looks a bit like a combination of the Info Line and the Key editor. A difference you should notice right away, however, is that information is displayed vertically instead of horizontally (as it is in the Key editor, project window, and Drum editor). What you might *not* notice right away is that what was the Note display should now be referred to as the *Event display* because it displays a box for *multiple* events, including note, pitch-bend, controller, program-change, aftertouch, poly-pressure, SMF (standard MIDI file), and score data. That's a lot of data to display! Another difference is that on the left side of your screen, instead of having a keyboard, track names, or drum names, the List editor contains information for each event in the Event display. This list is called the *info list*.

Zoom in on the Event display so that only one measure is visible. You can resize the info list by clicking and dragging the line that separates the info list from the Event display to the left or right. If you drag the separation line to the right, you'll see as many as 10 columns of information in the info list display, including L, Type, Start, End, Length, Data 1, Data 2, Data 3, Channel, and

Comment. You can change the order of these columns by dragging and dropping them between other columns, much as you could change the drum-map fields within the Drum editor.

To see the info list and Event display in action, click the Solo Edit and Autoscroll toolbar buttons and hit Play on the transport. You'll see a lot of information scroll by in the info list, and a lot of events scroll by in the Event display. Even though the bass part you're hearing sounds fairly simple, the multitude of events you're seeing makes it look very complex. That's because you're not only seeing note information, you're also seeing pitch-bend, multiple-controller, aftertouch, poly-pressure, and program-change data for this part.

Toolbar Overview

Just looking over the toolbar, you'll probably notice that several of the tools found in other editors are missing. For example, there's no Info Line in the toolbar because the List editor features the aforementioned info list on the left side of the screen. Additionally, no Glue, Split, or Line tool buttons are present. That said, the List editor's toolbar does contain some tools with which you are already familiar, and those tools works the same way here as in the Key editor, Drum editor, or project window.

As for tools in the List editor with which you are unfamiliar, here's a run-down:

- **Insert Type.** You can work with more than just note events in the List editor's Event display, which means you need some way to specify which type of event you want to create when you add an event with the Pencil tool. To do so, you use the Insert Type drop-down list. From this list, you can choose to create one of nine types of events: note, controller, program-change, aftertouch, poly-pressure, pitch-bend, Sys Ex data, SMF data, and text data.

- **Filter View.** When you click this viewing button, one of three available from the List editor's toolbar (see Figure 11.1), a Filter View field with options opens underneath the toolbar, much as the Info Line appears in the Key editor when Show Info Line is selected. The Filter View field enables you to remove various event options from the display in order to better focus on those events with which you're currently working. This can be very helpful, seeing as how so many events appear in the Event display at one time. To activate an event filter, simply click the checkbox next to the event type you'd like to remove from view to select it. (Note that the events will not be deleted or silenced in this process, just removed from the display.) When Filter View is deactivated, the Filter View field closes, but the settings will remain. That is, the view will still reflect the event options that have been checked.

Figure 11.1

From left to right: the Filter View button, the Mask View menu, and the Value View button.

■ **Value View.** If you think the Value View button must show you the lowest *priced* events, you're wrong. Instead, it opens a display on the right side of your screen (similar to the inspector in the project window, except on the other side of your display) that shows the numeric values (from one of the value columns in the list display) in bar-graph form (similar to the way velocities are displayed in a controller lane). You can edit within the Value View display in a similar way you edit velocities within a controller lane, except you're limited to only using the Pencil tool. Indeed, the OST automatically changes into the Pencil tool when it is positioned over the Value View display.

> **NOTE**
>
> The tricky thing about using the Value View display is that because it covers all the different types of events, the bar graph works on different types of values for the events. That means sometimes the bar graph reflects the values of the Data 1 column of the info list, while other times it reflects the values in the Data 2 column, depending on the type of event, and so on. For the most part, what's shown here is determined based on what makes sense to show in bar-graph form. For instance, a controller would display its controller amount within the Value View field as opposed to the controller type. But if you get confused, check out the chart on page 329 of the Cubase manual.

■ **Mask View.** The most complex view tool in the List editor's toolbar is the Mask View menu. You use it to hide all events from the Event display that don't meet the criteria you specify. This works well if, for instance, you want to isolate one particular type of controller instead of showing all the controller types. The Mask View menu is divided into two sections, one of which is a duplicate of the controls in the Logical editor (you'll learn more about those later in this chapter). When you don't need to hide any events from view, the Mask View menu should be set at Nothing. Otherwise, in order to use any of the other options in the menu, you must first select an event with which you want to work in the editor; then select the Event Types option in the Mask View menu. Everything will be removed from the display except events that share the same properties as the selected event. Selecting Event Types and Data 1 hides everything that isn't the same event type and doesn't have the same value in the Data 1 column as the event you have selected. If the events are set to separate MIDI channels within the part, you can use the Event Channels option to display all the events on the same MIDI channels as the event you have selected. This is particularly handy when you're working with multiple parts at once or when you have performed a Merge MIDI in Loop operation on all your MIDI tracks.

Event Types

I modified the Bass track so that it would show a lot more events than normal by adding some pitch bend, a program change, some aftertouch and poly-pressure, some MIDI panning, and some modulation. As a result, there are a lot more non-note events happening than note events. I did this because you've already discovered how and where to edit note information: in the Key editor. Very rarely will you need to edit a note within the List editor. Rather, the List editor is best at handling everything that *isn't* a note.

The Song12 demo captures a lot of types of events, but not all. The types it doesn't include are SMF, Sys Ex, and text data. Following is a brief explanation of those three types of events and how and where you might use them:

- **SMF.** Standard MIDI file (SMF) data is used primarily when you're creating a MIDI file that contains multiple MIDI channels and is something that you plan to share with other MIDI users. There are 128 specific types of data you can create or modify within the SMF fields, including a sequence number, copyright information, a track name, an instrument name, a lyric, marker info, cue points, key signature, and MIDI channel, with the remaining types being events. When you have an SMF data file in place, you can alter the type by changing the value in the List editor's Data 1 field. With the desired SMF data type selected, most of the settings are established simply by selecting the comment field and entering a number or name in it. When it comes to editing events in the SMF data field, you have to enter the necessary information in hexadecimal form (MIDI's basic language—not for the MIDI amateur). As you may have already guessed, working with SMF data is very technical, and most of the time it's not required unless you're specifically sharing files with someone. If you're planning on arranging MIDI parts for web sites, downloads, cell phones, game systems, or toy manufacturers (I'm sure I'm forgetting a few others), then you probably should take the time to explore SMF data, but it's not required if you simply want to create music in Cubase.

- **Text data.** This data is used to add lyrics or comments to a score. Using the List editor makes it easy to specify where you'd like the text to begin within the song. Once you've created a text event, you can type your text in the Comment field; you can also edit your comments by typing in the Text field in the Score editor. (I cover the Score editor in Chapter 12, "The Score Editor.")

- **Sys Ex data.** This type of data is not as scary as it sounds. Sys Ex, short for System Exclusive, is code that is embedded into all MIDI instruments and is designed to lay out the details of that instrument. The most basic usage of Sys Ex is to control patch data (the presets) within an individual synth. Owners of multi-timbral synths (synths that can play several sounds at one time) use Sys Ex messages to load their patch setup information into Cubase by recording the Sys Ex message into a MIDI sequence from their synths via a bulk Sys Ex dump; then, whenever they play that sequence back in Cubase, the Sys Ex message is sent from Cubase to set up the parameters of the synth. This takes the pain out of having to set up your instruments and patches every time you load your song into Cubase. In addition, depending on the synth you're using, you may be able to send messages from the synth to Cubase regarding changes you make via the controls on that synth (sliders, knobs, and so on) through Sys

Ex so that the filters or changes you make to your synth's sound during a performance are recorded as well as the notes and controller data. When you select a Sys Ex event in the List editor and then click the Comments field, the Sys Ex editor opens (see Figure 11.2); this looks very similar to what you see when editing an SMF event.

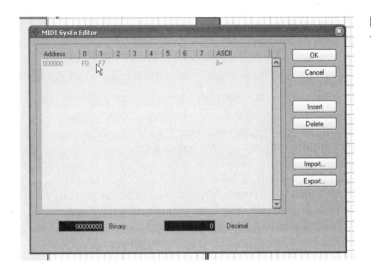

Figure 11.2

The Sys Ex editor.

> **NOTE**
>
> Most people who use Sys Ex do so strictly for the basics, but if you need to get more technical, you can edit Sys Ex data in hexadecimal within the Sys Ex editor. For more information, see the Cubase manual; it devotes an entire chapter to working with Sys Ex messages. Also, read up on sending and receiving Sys Ex messages via MIDI in your synth's manual.

> **TIP**
>
> If you're not using a multi-timbral synth, or if you're only using one particular sound from an individual synth, I recommend using a program change as opposed to sending Sys Ex messages to and from Cubase. Program changes offer the same result, with a lot less complication. And if you're only using VST instruments, there is no need for sending or receiving Sys Ex messages at all; that's because the settings and automation of the VST instrument are automatically saved within a project. Indeed, with the invention of VST instruments, the need for Sys Ex messages has diminished.

As for the types of events that do appear in the demo song, allow me to briefly explain how each event type works:

■ **Note events.** Working with a note event in the List editor is very similar to working with a note in the Key editor. The info list displays the note-event information very much like the Info Line displays the note info within the Key editor. The Start, End, and Length fields are identical to their corresponding fields on the Info Line. The Data 1 field represents the note number of the event, the Data 2 field represents the Velocity value of the event, and the Data 3 field represents the Off Velocity value of the event. Finally, the Channel field defines the MIDI channel for that particular event. Unlike some of the other event types, there is no use for the Comment field when working with note events.

■ **Controller events.** A controller event has only a start location; it has no end or length locations. The Data 1 field represents the type of controller event (pan, modulation, volume, and so on), and the Data 2 field represents the Amount setting of that controller. The Channel field represents the MIDI channel on which the controller event will be sent out. The Data 3 and Comment fields have no use in the info list when working with a controller event.

■ **Program-change event.** A program change is technically a controller command, but it's been separated by Cubase into its own group so that the info fields can work better with it. Like the controller event, a program-change event only has a start location. The Data 1 field displays the program number that will be sent out to the synth (therefore changing the synth's current program setting), but the Data 2 and Data 3 fields have no apparent use. (You can, however, change the numbers in the Data 2 field, so it's possible that this could have an effect on a program change.) The Channel field represents the MIDI channel on which the program change will be sent out. The Comment field has no use with a program-change event.

NOTE

The tricky thing about working with program changes is that synth preset numbers sometimes don't match MIDI program numbers. The easiest way to find the program number is to select the program-change event with the OST and then scroll through the program numbers while watching your synth. The patches will change on your synth as you scroll through the program numbers. When you arrive at the correct patch, you've arrived at the correct program number.

NOTE

Because VST instruments often have to load their programs or samples from the hard drive, there are sometimes no preset numbers to work with. If this is the case, a program change will be ineffective. The only two VST instruments that come with Cubase and enable you to use program changes are the Monologue and Embracer VST synths.

■ **Aftertouch and poly-pressure events.** Aftertouch and poly-pressure are two other controller event types that require their own grouping because of how their data is handled. *Aftertouch* (also known as *channel aftertouch*) is an effect that some keyboards have that enables the performer to alter the sound by applying pressure to a key after it's been pressed. *Poly-pressure* (also referred to as *polyphonic aftertouch*) enables a user to apply pressure on several different key at one time, creating a different sound alteration to each key that has been pressed. When a keyboard has only aftertouch, the sound alteration occurs to the sound of every key that's pressed instead of each individual key. (It's important to know that not only does a keyboard have to be specially designed to create this effect, but the playback synth also has to be programmed and designed to re-create the effect after it's been recorded in a sequence. Otherwise, the recorded effect will not be heard.) An aftertouch event uses only the Start field, the Data 1 field, and the Channel field. The Data 1 field contains the amount of the aftertouch effect, and the Channel field captures the output MIDI channel. A poly-pressure event's Start and Channel fields work the same as when working with an aftertouch event. Its Data 1 field contains the note number that is affected, and its Data 2 field captures the amount of the effect on that particular note number. The poly-pressure and aftertouch events I've created within this part are for reference only and have no effect on the sound whatsoever, due to the fact that the sound and synth do not respond to either aftertouch or poly-pressure.

■ **Pitch-bend events.** Because you explored pitch bend in the controller lane of the Key editor, you should be aware that pitch bend is also another (continuous) controller event. The reason pitch bend gets its own grouping is due to the fact that it can contain a much larger number (in the thousands) of increments, unlike other controller events. The pitch-bend event uses only the Start, Data 1, and Channel fields. The Data 1 field captures the pitch-bend amount, and the Channel field displays the MIDI output for the pitch-bend effect.

Creating and Editing Events in the Event Display

Although the List editor can be used to create events, I often find that creating note, pitch-bend, (most) controller, aftertouch, and poly-pressure events is easier within the other editors. For example, pitch-bend, aftertouch, and poly-pressure events are usually created by the keyboard controller that has been used to create a part. In contrast, the List editor works best when you need to edit an event type such as a program change, SMF data, or a text element.

I find it easiest to edit all events by first selecting the event type I'd like to edit and then using the Mask View function, selecting either Event Types or Event Types and Data 1. That way, I'm only viewing one particular controller. Then I can use the Value View display to do some quick overall edits if necessary. Figure 11.3 shows the same part with the pitch-bend displayed, using the Mask View Event Types option and some quick changes made with the Pencil tool in the Value View display.

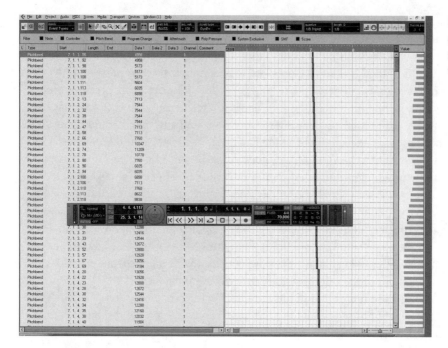

Figure 11.3

Concentrating on editing pitch-bend events in the List editor.

Creating a Program Change

To create a program change in the List editor, select Program Change from the Insert Event menu and use the Pencil tool to create an event in the Event display at the location where you want a program change. (Note that it's a good idea to start the program change one measure before your next note is played within the part because sometimes program changes are delayed or cause glitches in a synth's performance.)

> **NOTE**
>
> When creating a program change, it's important to know that after you change a program, it won't change back unless there's another program change. That means if you want to have a program change later during a song, you should also insert a program change with the default program at the start of a song so that when you play the song a second time, the program will reset to its original program. Notice how I inserted a program change before the bass part that includes the program number of the original part; then, later in the song, I inserted another program change to alter the sound at the end of the part.

Adding SMF Data

Most basic SMF data comments are inserted at the start of a MIDI file. Creating a SMF data comment works the same way as creating a program change works, except you select SMF from the

Insert Event menu instead of Program Change. After the event has been inserted, you can edit the fields in whichever way necessary.

> **TIP**
>
> The arrow in the L column on the far left end of the info list represents the position of the cursor as it scrolls through the song. If you'd like to start the playback of the song from a particular event in the part, simply double-click the field box in the L column to the left of the event listed in the info list.

Adding Text Elements to a Score

Text comments can be added to the score in the same way as SMF data is added to a MIDI file, except instead of choosing SMF from the Insert Event menu, you select Text. When you have the text event in the appropriate location, you can type whatever you'd like in the Comment field. (Note that if there are a lot of words—for example, if you're adding lyrics—I find it easier to add the extra words within the Score editor.)

The Logical Editor

The Logical editor enables you to create complex formulas to search out and alter MIDI data in a multitude of ways. The Transformer MIDI effect and the MIDI Input Transformer option (both found in the MIDI effects and the inspector's display) are just real-time representations of the Logical editor. When I say *real-time*, I mean that even though you *hear* the effect of the Logical editor, the actual events are not altered until they are processed using the Freeze MIDI Modifiers function.

The Logical editor can be accessed from several places within Cubase. The most direct way of accessing the Logical editor is by opening the MIDI menu and selecting Logical Editor. You can also access the Logical editor from the List editor by selecting Setup from the Mask View menu.

The Mask View and MIDI menus also offer a number of presets that are used in conjunction with the Logical editor. They are listed in Added for Version 3, Experimental, Standard Set 1, and Standard Set 2 submenus, with each heading capturing a number of presets to use. These presets are also displayed in the Logical editor's Preset menu (see Figure 11.4). An Init setting is also available, used to erase any current setting within the Logical editor so that you can start with a clean slate.

Because using the Logical editor can become pretty technical, I highly recommend that beginners stick with the presets until they feel like they need to take things farther.

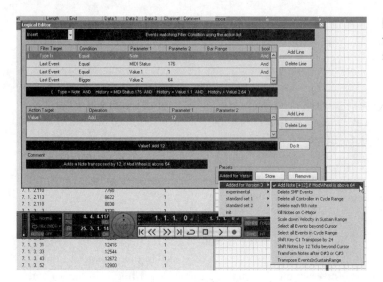

Figure 11.4

The Logical editor, displaying a few of its presets.

You use the Logical editor by first selecting the part or notes in the project window or in some other editor that you want to edit. (If you don't select a particular part or group of notes, all parts or notes displayed in the current window will be affected. Unless you're prepared to change the entire part or project, make sure you have a group of notes or a part selected.) Then, open the Logical editor. When creating a formula in the Logical editor, the first step is to set filter conditions that determine the events on which you will be performing an edit in the selected part. After you determine the note or notes you will be affecting, you then decide what action you want to perform on those events. The final step depends on which action you choose, but in some cases it's required to define the action in further detail.

To help you understand the concept a little better, here's a very simplified analogy for this complicated editor. Say you have three people: Tom, Oscar, and Aretha (notes/events). The first step would be selecting Oscar (the event/note). The second step would be telling him to jump (the action). The last step would be telling him how high and which direction to jump—say, backward three feet.

The great thing about working with the Logical editor is that you can affect a large group of notes/events at one time. Of course, if you want to take action on only specific notes, you must be very thorough in describing which note/events you would like to affect. For instance, since it's not likely that a lot of the notes will be named Oscar, as in the previous analogy, I would need to set up more specific guidelines that describe the note I'm looking for. Using a similar analogy, instead of selecting only Oscar out of a large group of people, I could select only the males with brown hair between the ages of 25 and 30, over 5'6", and under 200 lbs.

The good news is you can get very creative with these filtering conditions. The bad news is that you have to sort of think like a MIDI mathematician in order to achieve the desired effect. Indeed, the Cubase manual has devoted a whole chapter to the Logical editor. Because this book can't go into a lot of detail without getting overly technical, I highly recommend that you take time to study that section of the manual, which is also available in PDF format via the Cubase Help menu.

Making the Logical Editor's Presets Your Own

When you use the Logical editor's presets from the MIDI menu or the Mask View menu, the preset is applied to the MIDI part immediately, bypassing the Logical editor. This can be convenient if the preset is exactly what you need as is. But by first opening the Logical editor and then selecting a preset from the Preset menu, you can see the workings of the preset and even alter the preset's formula to better suit your needs.

To get the hang of this, do the following:

1. Close the current song and open Song13 from the CD-ROM that accompanies this book.

2. Open the Logical editor and select the Delete Each 5th Note preset from the Added for Version 3 submenu. This preset has been formulated to remove every fifth note in the sequence. (This preset is interesting because it doesn't matter how many notes there are in the selected part or on what beat the note falls within the song.)

3. Select Do It to remove every fifth note of the current part.

4. Undo the change to restore the file to its original state.

5. Although there isn't a preset for removing every other note, you can modify the Delete Each 5th Note preset to remove every other note. To do so, change the value in the Parameter 2 line from 5 to 2 (see Figure 11.5).

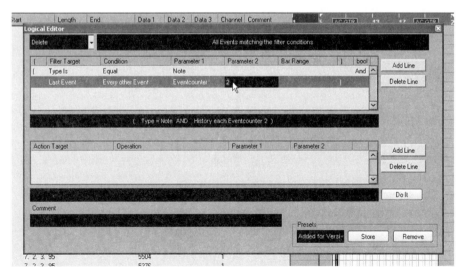

Figure 11.5

Alter the Delete Each 5th Note preset to instead delete every other note.

6. Click Do It.

7. Play back the arpeggio guitar part to hear that every other note has been removed, creating more of a half-time feel.

8. Select the Downbeat Accent (4-4) preset from the Experimental submenu. This preset was cleverly designed to increase the velocity of every downbeat (in a song in 4/4 time).

9. Look at the Action Target setting; you will see that Value 2 (which in this case represents the note's velocity) will *increase* the downbeat (Add) by 30 (Parameter 1's setting). The downbeat is selected by the complex formula located in the top half of the Logical editor. To soften the downbeats instead of increasing their velocity, change the Operation setting to Subtract (instead of Add) and change the Parameter 1 setting to 65.

10. Click Do It.

11. Listen to the changes. As you do, examine the velocities in the Value View window to see how each downbeat is now lower than the upbeats (see Figure 11.6).

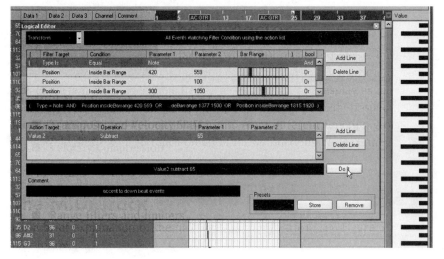

Figure 11.6

Change the Downbeat Accent (4-4) preset to lower each downbeat's velocity instead of accenting the velocity.

12. Select the Set Notes to Fixed Pitch (c3) preset from the Standard Set 2 submenu. This preset has been designed to change the pitch of all the selected notes to C3. Of course, even if you want all your notes to be the same pitch, you might not necessarily want that pitch to be C3. In this case, the Value 1 setting represents a note event. The action that the Logical editor takes is to set each note event to a fixed value, which is represented in Parameter 1 as 60. The number 60 translates to C3. Because there are 12 steps between each octave, if you wanted the fixed value to become C2, you would change the number to 48.

13. In this case, change the fixed note to G3. To do so, change the Parameter 1 value to 67.

14. Click Do It.

15. Play back the track; every note is a G3. Also notice that every note's Data 1 column in the List editor reads G3 (see Figure 11.7).

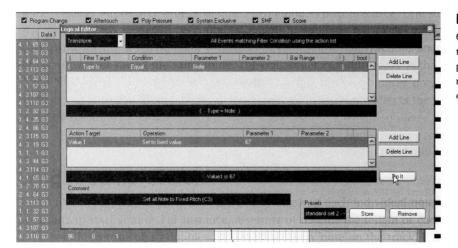

Figure 11.7

Change the Set Notes to Fixed Pitch (c3) preset to change the notes to a fixed pitch of G3.

NOTE

After you modify a preset, I recommend saving that preset and describing its function in the preset name. You will find that this will save you a lot of time with future edits.

Knowing the effect or edit you would like to create and knowing how to program the Logical editor so that it will give you the result you're looking for can be tricky. Again, I recommend reading the Cubase manual's chapter on the Logical editor if you get serious about creating your own presets.

NOTE

As mentioned earlier, the Logical editor, the Transformer, and the Input Transformer all work in very similar ways. The main differences are that the Logical editor works best as an editor (to change the note), the Transformer works as an effect (to process the notes without changing them), and when you record or play through the Input Transformer, the edit occurs as you are playing or recording the part in Cubase. That means you bypass the original part altogether, skipping straight to the processed part. For musicians using Cubase in live performance, this could create some pretty radical effects. The Logical Editor, Transformer, and Input Transformer all have minor differences, and the Cubase manual goes over these differences in detail if you wish to dig deeper into them.

The Project Browser

The Project browser is an editor that works with MIDI, audio, automation, the tempo/time signature tracks, video, and markers within the currently open project (song). Working with MIDI in the Project browser is like working with a combination of the List editor and Windows Explorer or Mac OS X Finder. Even though it doesn't come close to offering the detail of the List editor, the Project browser can provide a quick list overview for the entire song, which is something the List editor can't do quite as well.

For a quick tour of the MIDI side of the Project browser, first close any songs you might have open and open Song14 on the CD-ROM accompanying this book. Then open the Project menu (located on the menu bar) and select Browser. (Alternatively, press Ctrl+B on your computer keyboard.)

Because you're working only with MIDI tracks, there will be no audio tracks present. If there were audio tracks, you would see them represented along with the MIDI tracks in this window, just as you would within the project window, except they would appear in a list fashion (like the MIDI files are shown). The left column of the Project browser should show all the track names, with each of the MIDI tracks represented by a MIDI symbol (see Figure 11.8). Here's a run-down on how to use the Project browser:

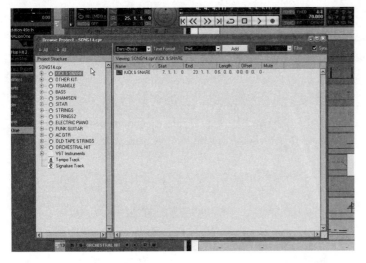

Figure 11.8

The Project browser window displaying all the MIDI tracks in the left column.

■ Clicking the plus sign (+) next to each track will reveal the parts on that track. You can also click +All above the Project Structure column to expand the view on all the tracks at once. Clicking –All or the minus sign (–) next to a track (after the tracks have been expanded) collapses the view to again show only the tracks.

■ If a MIDI track is selected, it's possible to add a part to the selected track. Creating a part in this way places an empty part between the left and right locators within the track. To create the blank part, simply select Add from over the Event display on the right and the new part will be created. Add is the only selection type available while working with MIDI tracks in the Project browser.

■ The Time Format menu, located over the Event display, is used only to define how the time reference is displayed in the Event display.

■ The Filter menu works much like the Filter View menu works in the List editor when you're working with MIDI events in parts, except you can only filter one particular type of event at once as opposed to being able to filter multiple types. (This filter menu has no use when working with tracks.)

■ You might check the Sync Selection checkbox when simultaneously using the project window with the Project browser. That way, everything you select within the project window will also be selected within the Project browser (and vice versa). You'll probably want to keep this box checked most of the time because it's a handy feature when working with the Project browser.

■ When a MIDI track has been expanded to show its parts, and a part has been selected from within that MIDI track, the MIDI events of the selected track are displayed in the Event display. Shown in Figure 11.9 is the bass part (from the Bass track), displaying its events in the Event display in a way very similar to the List editor.

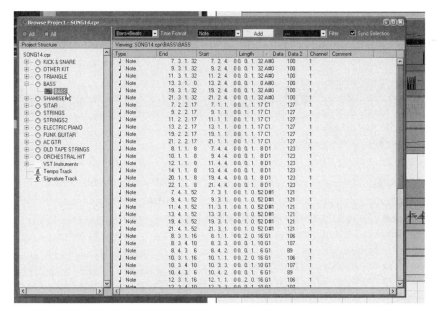

Figure 11.9

The bass part, displayed in the Project browser.

■ You can insert new events in the Project browser by first selecting the type of event from the menu located just to the left of the Add button, moving the cursor in the project window to the position where you want to insert the event, and clicking the Add button within the

Project browser. This is very similar to inserting an event within the List editor, except you don't have the tool buttons to help you, and you have to use the cursor in the project window to mark your place.

■ If you need detailed MIDI editing, the List editor is still the best place to make your adjustments. However, the Project browser allows you to jump quickly from part to part if you are working with multiple parts at the same time. By using the Project Structure column with your track view expanded so that you can see all your parts, you can effortlessly navigate from (for instance) the bass part to the sitar part by simply clicking the necessary part (see Figure 11.10).

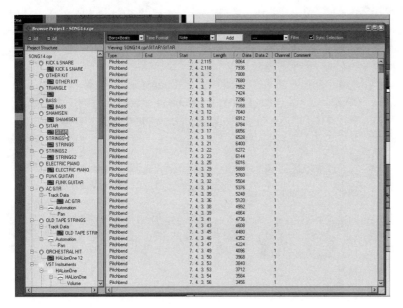

Figure 11.10

Switching to edit another part is really simple in the Project browser.

■ As in the List editor and Drum editor, you can change the order of your columns using the drag-and-drop method. You can also resize your columns by dragging the divider lines between them. By clicking in the desired column heading, you can also change the order in which events are displayed (similar to the Arrange By feature in Windows Explorer).

12 The Score Editor

Y ou've spent days editing your MIDI recording to perfection, and it sounds amazing. You put out the record, and it sells millions of copies. Everybody loves your song. Your publisher's contact calls you and says he needs your song in printed sheet music form, ASAP. A representative from a major motion-picture studio calls to tell you she wants to score the film with your song, but she needs you to orchestrate it because the song needs to be performed with live studio musicians. You panic, because you've never scored for live musicians before, and you can't even read sheet music. But wait—you remember that you can print a score from Cubase. You pull up the Score editor by opening the MIDI menu and choosing Open Score Editor, print out some sheet music, and send it to the publisher and studio. During the recording session, however, the studio representative calls and asks, "Are you sure this is right? This sounds like garbage!" So you check your backup copies against what appears on the screen, and everything matches. The sequence still sounds amazing. You call the studio back and tell her to get better musicians, but she says she hired the best musicians in town. What happened?

Here's what happened: You can print sheet music from Cubase's Score editor, but MIDI recordings and a printed score don't exactly go hand in hand. Here's why: Even though you can technically edit MIDI using the Score editor, it is not considered a MIDI editor. Instead, Cubase defines it as a MIDI *interpreter*. That is, it translates a MIDI recording into what it thinks you are trying to say musically and throws it up on your screen in sheet-music format. So even though Cubase has all the tools you need to create a professional score, obtaining the perfect score isn't as easy as clicking Print Score. In fact, creating the perfect score can sometimes take longer than actually recording and editing the MIDI parts.

Understanding the Score Editor

If you know and understand MIDI, and you understand how to read, write, and arrange music for live performance, then the Score editor is for you. If you don't know how to read sheet music, then the Score editor is not for you at all. To get a sense of what the Score editor does, close any songs you might have open in Cubase and open Song15 from the CD-ROM accompanying this book.

All the tracks of the demo song I've created for this book appear in the Score editor. More precisely, what you are seeing is the demo song as translated by the Score editor into sheet-music form. If you don't know how to read sheet music, this might look a lot like other sheet music you've seen. If you *do* know how to read sheet music, however, you will probably see that although a lot of what you see makes sense, some parts of the score don't look right. In fact, it looks a lot harder to read than it should, seeing as how it's a fairly simple piece of music.

The trick to creating sheet music that works is being able to determine how the piece will sound just by reading the sheet music. The sound you hear from the MIDI playback has little to do with how the actual sheet music will sound when professional musicians read the score and play what they're reading. Indeed, composers and arrangers usually study for years so that they understand every acoustic musical instrument, its note range, and the way each note should sound when played on the instrument. They also understand the way in which musicians need to see music in order to get the results they want. Before a score is even handed to a musician, the composer or arranger likely has a fairly good idea of how the entire score should sound when played. Although last-minute corrections might sometimes be made during a live playdown, with the part simply modified by hand, every second counts when you have an 80-piece orchestra and they're all getting paid scale. You just don't have time on location to go back into Cubase and make corrections.

An Overview of the Capabilities of the Score Editor

Because the Score editor is not really a MIDI editor, I don't go over it in detail in this book. Besides, the Score editor is so complex, 25 percent of the Cubase manual is dedicated to explaining how to edit a score using Cubase. This says a lot, since coverage of the Key editor accounts for less than 5 percent of the Cubase manual. That said, I do take the time to go over the capabilities of the Score editor for those of you who are interested in learning how to use this powerful tool. They are as follows:

■ The Score editor can work completely independently of the MIDI tracks you have created. After you create a score, you can quantize the way notes are displayed on the sheet music without affecting the position of the notes in the sequence. This is useful because more often than not, something that sounds great during MIDI playback may not be readable by your average musician through its automatic translation into the Score editor. A good arranger understands that the more difficult a part is for a musician to follow, the harder it will be for the musician to perform the music the way it was intended. The Score editor includes a display quantize for both notes and rests, which works by limiting the note value that can be displayed. That means, for example, that if a note falls slightly ahead of or is held a little longer than a quarter note, instead of Cubase calling it a dotted quarter note or a 32nd note tied to a quarter note, the note will appear as simply a quarter note, making the read a lot easier.

■ You can enter notes into the Score editor by hand as opposed to using a MIDI keyboard. More than likely, you'll find that both using a MIDI keyboard *and* sometimes entering notes by hand is the way to go.

■ Each track in Cubase represents a solo instrument. By selecting multiple tracks and parts before opening the Score editor, you create a score with each individual track (instrument) receiving its own stave. If you're creating a score that will be played by multiple musicians, you'll often want to create a printout of each individual track for each player, as well as a copy that contains all parts staved together for the conductor.

NOTE

When you're creating sheet music for piano, there is usually a treble clef stave and a bass clef stave. For this reason, the Score editor allows you to split a single piano track into two staves.

■ Viewing a large score can be a challenge in itself. For this reason, the Score editor has two modes for viewing: Edit mode and Page mode. Edit mode, the default mode, displays the work area in a way that's similar to the other editors, while Page mode displays an entire page of music at once. As shown in Figure 12.1, you can scroll through these pages much as you would scroll through the pages of a document in a program such as Microsoft Word.

NOTE

When Page mode is disabled, you are working in the default Edit mode.

Figure 12.1

Using Page mode in the Score editor.

- You can create chord and guitar symbols in a variety of ways over the staff. Time and key signatures can also be added (as they should!). It's possible to transpose instrument parts (such as brass instruments) without affecting the actual MIDI part.

- You can add triplets where the program has translated the part into something other than triplets, consolidate rests so that the music uses dotted rests instead of multiple rests, and fix incorrect note lengths and overlaps—all without affecting the original MIDI track.

- You can determine how notes, such as 1/8 notes or 1/16 notes, are beamed together. You can also change a note's stem flag position and determine how polyphonic voices (multiple notes or chords) are displayed.

- You can create guitar tablature for your printed score, adding symbols, lyrics, accidentals, grace notes, and a whole lot more. Indeed, virtually every symbol you can think of from sheet music you've read is available in the Score editor. You can alter these symbols (such as dynamic symbols) so that they fit over or under the notes in the appropriate positions.

- You can split any MIDI track into multiple instrument staves using a function called Explode. This comes in handy when you want to divide a chord (which might have been played over a mono instrument's part) into multiple instruments so that the same result can be achieved with live musicians.

- Although you can use the List editor to add a text event, adding and editing text events is even easier within the Score editor. You can position the words in relation to where the notes fall on the staff, which is how lyrics and music are typically written in sheet music. You can also change the text's font and font size.

NOTE

Even though Cubase's text functions are quite impressive, there are more limitations than you might find in a program like Microsoft Word. For instance, there is no spell check available. The good news is you can easily copy and paste your text from a Word document (or any text document) into a text line in the Score editor.

- You can automatically number your bars in the Score editor. Numbered bars are common for large playdowns or studio environments because the composer or conductor can use the numbers as an easy reference when navigating different parts of the music. You can also determine how many bars you would like to show per line of music. When you're dealing with bars that contain a lot of notes, it is good practice to use fewer bars per line as opposed to trying to cram everything on one page. Then again, having too many pages can also result in a difficult reading—for example, it's hard for players to turn pages when both their hands are used on their instrument, which can result in a dropped note or other type of mistake—so sometimes it's good to use as many bars per line as possible.

■ The Score editor enables you to set up score layouts, applying settings such as bar spacing, symbols, vertical spacing, and so on. This can make things easier if you're editing a lot of the same types of scores. The Score editor also boasts an Auto Layout feature, which works like the display quantize except with bars, staves, and pages instead of notes. A layout can be saved for an individual instrument or an entire score.

■ Writing for drums or percussion is different from writing for a melodic instrument. For one thing, the pitch references on the staff have no meaning to a drummer. That's why, when you worked in the Drum editor, you came across symbols for drum note heads within the Drum Map Setup dialog box. Cubase uses *head pairs* for drummers to symbolize different types of drums and different note lengths played on drums. An empty head symbolizes a 1/2 or whole note-length value, while a filled head symbolizes 1/4 notes and shorter-length notes (indicated by their flags). The default head pairs are commonly used when writing drum or percussion parts, but an arranger can modify these to his liking. I've seen keys that define which drums are at which pitch with which note head written on scores, but it's usually easy for a drum-kit or percussion player to determine which note is for which particular drum or cymbal in a kit.

■ After you have set up your score with all the appropriate dynamic symbols, it's possible to hear dynamic results played back via MIDI by defining what the values of the symbols are. This is like editing MIDI with the Score editor without actually editing the MIDI, but more so processing the MIDI so that it sounds as if it has been edited. This was designed so that those who wish to create a score from scratch from within the Score editor can alter dynamics without opening the other editors. Personally, I feel this is a waste of time because there are too many factors that determine what sounds good with MIDI; the best way to control the sound is by editing the MIDI in the MIDI editors, as covered in previous chapters, or by working directly with the synth or sampler parameters. My point is that if you really want the most accurate and best *sound*, you should work in the other editors.

■ Printing your finished score is easy. To do so, switch to Page mode in the Score editor, open the File menu, and select Print. You can also export the score as a JPEG, BMP, GIF, TIF, or PNG file, which you can then open and edit in other programs such as Photoshop, Word, or FrontPage.

Overall, Cubase 4 has some amazing Score editor features. Indeed, the Score editor has become a very valuable tool for editing a score. For those of you who read music and want to provide music to live musicians, I highly recommend reading up on the Score editor in the Cubase manual or in another book solely devoted to editing a score in Cubase. If you've used other programs, such as Finale, you may find some elements of the Score editor are easier to work with, especially when used to edit a score you created using Cubase.

If you're mostly working with synths and samplers, as opposed to live musicians, and you have no need to print sheet music, there's no need to bother with the Score editor. Even though it's a powerful score-editing tool, it is the most difficult MIDI editor to use and doesn't offer the flexibility of the other MIDI editors. Because Cubase has so much to offer, I recommend that you prioritize your learning experience, focusing first on understanding more about the virtual instruments, automation, and audio-editing capabilities before you tackle the scoring side, which may not be necessary for you anyway.

13

Now That You Know Everything There Is to Know about Editing MIDI in Cubase . . .

Although this book covers every way you can edit MIDI in Cubase, it barely scratches the surface of some of the editors. In fact, it didn't even *touch* more than half of the program's functions. If you're already familiar with the rest of the program, and you just wanted to learn more about the MIDI side, you have accomplished your goal. If, however, you haven't explored the rest of Cubase, I highly recommend that you take the time to master it to the extent that you have mastered the MIDI side. Doing so will only help you down the road. Whatever your circumstances, it's important that you put the knowledge you've gained from this book to good use again and again. Practice makes perfect; the more you use the program, the faster and better you'll become at it.

Exporting Your MIDI File to Audio

As you've learned, there's a lot you can do with MIDI. But if you add the power of digital audio to your MIDI knowledge, the sky is the limit. The following exercise demonstrates how to export your MIDI file to an audio file. After you create an audio file, you can then edit the file even further using Cubase's audio-editing tools. Then, when you're satisfied with every aspect of the song, you can output the file as a stereo mix, which you can burn onto a CD or convert into an MP3 so that the rest of the world can hear your masterpiece.

1. Close any songs you might have open in Cubase and load Song17 from the CD-ROM that accompanies this book.

2. Open the File menu, choose Export, and select Audio Mixdown. The Export Audio Mixdown dialog box opens.

3. Click the File Name field and type Skill Pack Song to change the file's name.

4. Click Choose. A browser-style window opens, where you can select the path to which your audio file will be exported.

5. Using Windows Explorer or Mac Finder, create a new folder on your hard drive, naming it "Skill Pack Demo."

6. In the browser-style window, click the Skill Pack Demo folder you just created.

7. Click Save. The settings in the Export Audio Mixdown dialog box should appear similar to those in Figure 13.1.

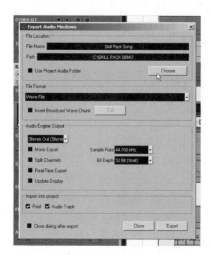

Figure 13.1

The Export Audio Mixdown dialog box.

8. Open the Audio Engine Output menu and choose Stereo Out.

9. Change the sample rate to 44.1 kHz (CD quality) and the bit depth to 32 bit (float).

10. Click the Import into Pool and Project checkboxes to select them.

11. Click Export. Cubase processes the audio export; when it is finished, an audio file appears below your MIDI files (see Figure 13.2).

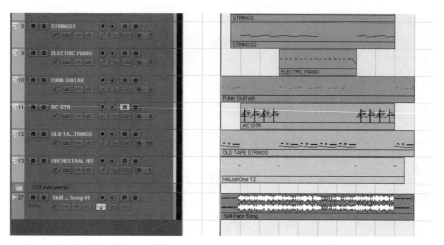

Figure 13.2

The audio file appears below the MIDI files on an audio track.

12. Click the Solo button on the audio track you just created and listen to your track. You should notice that it sounds the same, but what you're listening to is actually an audio recording of what you were hearing before.

13. Use the Split tool to cut the audio file at measure 6 and at measure 7, just as you would edit a MIDI file.

14. Using the OST, select the audio clip between measures 5 and 6.

15. Open the Audio menu, choose Process, and select Reverse.

16. Using the OST, select the audio clip between measures 6 and 7.

17. Open the Audio menu, choose Process, and select Pitch Shift. The Pitch Shift Settings dialog box opens.

18. In the Pitch Shift Settings dialog box, click the Envelope tab and select the first of the three curves.

19. Change the Range setting to 5 semitones.

20. Change the Transpose setting to 0 semitones.

21. Click Process. (This operation may take a moment.)

22. Listen to the newly edited song. This is a brief example of what you can accomplish knowing how to edit audio.

23. With the audio track still soloed, repeat steps 1–11, except this time change the song name to "Skill Pack Song Edit."

24. When the file appears under the previous one, mute the first file and solo the new one. When you play it back, you should hear a new mix of what you just created.

In this example, you created an audio file from a MIDI song, and then you edited the audio file and created a new mix of your edited audio file. These edits are among the simplest possible audio edits you can make in Cubase; they don't even *begin* to scratch the surface of what you can do when you incorporate digital audio with MIDI, not to mention the mixer, audio plug-in effects, and automation. Even so, I hope it gives you an idea of the power you can wield. When you master audio editing, you can correct the pitch of a vocal performance, correct the timing of a live bass player, make a 31-second song into a 29-second song, loop anything into a groove with an incredible feel, and much, much more. The good news is that simple audio part edits are done in a manner very similar to editing a MIDI part in the project window.

For a comparison of the audio files you created in the preceding exercise, you can import the WAV files with the same names as you used in the exercise from the Skill Pack Demo folder on the CD-ROM. For more information on importing audio files, refer to the Cubase manual.

Making Cubase Your Own

There are many ways to customize Cubase to make your working experience more enjoyable. Tailoring your workspace, creating project templates, and setting up your preferences can save you loads of time in the long run, enabling you to dive right into creating music rather than wasting a lot of time just trying to get Cubase up and running.

Tailoring Your Workspace

As you've probably noticed, you can have a lot of windows open in Cubase at one time—the editors, the mixer, effects, VST instruments, the Project browser, the transport, and so on. When you perform certain tasks, you might want your windows to appear a certain way in order to expedite your work. For instance, during mixdown, you might want to see your mixer, your VST instruments, the project window, and some audio plug-ins. Alternatively, when working on drums, you might want to see the Drum editor, a VST instrument panel, the project window, the transport, and the VST performance meter. Fortunately, Cubase enables you to tailor a workspace (that is, the visual layout of the program) to suit your needs. Customizing a workspace is like setting up your desk the way you like it. Specifically, you can determine which windows should be active, what size each window should be, and where each window should be located. After you have created the perfect workspace, you can then save it, opening it whenever you need to perform the task for which the workspace was created. Commands for creating and loading workspaces can be found under the Window menu; for more information on workspaces, see the Cubase manual.

Using a Project Template

Creating a project template is similar to setting up a workspace, except it sets up everything the way you like it from the start of a project. This can be very handy if, for example, you regularly use the same tools to create music. Using a project template, you can save all your track names, automatically load and set up your VST instruments and plug-in effects, determine what types of tracks you would like to display as well as how many of each type, and set up your windows exactly the way you like them—all at the start of a project. To set up a template, open the File menu and choose Save As Template. For more details, see the Cubase manual.

Setting Up Preferences

Setting up your preferences can also save you loads of time, as well as enable Cubase to work the way you want it to work. To set your preferences, open the File menu and choose Preferences; the dialog box that opens enables you to establish default Cubase settings (see Figure 13.3). For

184

example, you can establish how you want things to look in Cubase using the Appearance settings, how editors work using the Editors settings, how different types of events are displayed in the Event Display settings, and many more. I highly recommend that you take the time to browse all the preferences so you can get an idea of what can and can't be changed.

Figure 13.3

The Preferences dialog box.

Using the Media Bay

One of the newest additions to Cubase is the Media Bay, a powerful file-handling system you can use to browse, filter, and organize all the media files on your computer system. Those of you who have been doing this a while are likely very familiar with the problems associated with file management when you have thousands of samples and file types to sort through. Fortunately, the Media Bay is designed to make this task easier. If you're planning to use Cubase to its fullest potential, I highly recommend that you take the time to explore the Media Bay and read up on it in the Cubase manual.

You've Conquered MIDI Editing in Cubase!

Congratulations! I'm impressed. Cubase is a very complex program, and you've covered a lot of it. Here's the catch: Although Cubase has everything you need to create music, you will find that once you learn it all, you'll want even more. Fortunately, there are plenty of third-party developers out there to keep you satisfied for a long time.

First, you'll probably want to explore VST instruments. Steinberg offers many VST instruments that aren't included with Cubase, but that were designed for use with Cubase—meaning they usually integrate into Cubase very well. You can find these other plug-ins listed on Steinberg's web site. In addition to VST instruments by Steinberg, you'll also find some by other manufacturers. Indeed, because Cubase is such a popular program, most manufacturers design their VST instruments to work within Cubase.

In addition to exploring VST instruments, you can also explore audio-processing plug-ins. Even though Cubase 4 comes equipped with some excellent audio plug-ins, you may find that you need some others. One plug-in that Cubase doesn't offer is pitch-correction software, which is quickly becoming standard issue for vocalists these days. There are several pitch-correction programs on the market today; one of the most popular ones is the Antares Auto Tune plug-in. As you use your plug-ins more and more, you'll become aware of what additional types of plug-ins would be useful to you—and if you look hard enough, you'll find them.

Even though you can create music in Cubase, you may find you need to use additional programs, such as Reason. These other programs may offer more flexibility and inspiration than Cubase for the type of music you're writing. Fortunately, Steinberg is very aware that Cubase can't do it all, which is why it offers ReWire; it enables you to work with two programs simultaneously by sharing the audio engine of Cubase. Even if the other program doesn't use ReWire, you can always export your file in a format that Cubase understands, such as a standard MIDI file or one of many different types of audio files. You can also import and export OMF (Open Media Framework) so that you can use Cubase files with other popular programs such as Pro Tools or Logic and vice versa.

Lastly, if you step outside of your computer for a moment, you'll find an infinite number of musical instruments and hardware processors that you can use with Cubase. Indeed, seeing as this book is based on MIDI, you probably already have some external MIDI keyboards or instruments.

NOTE

There are plenty of ways to change your work environment between your external synth or sampler and Cubase, but sometimes what you may need to change involves knowing the inner workings of your instrument itself.

The important thing to realize is that even though Cubase is a big part of the picture, the big picture involves a whole lot more than just Cubase. The other thing to keep in mind is that because technology is always developing, all these programs will evolve and change over time— which means you must evolve and change as well. If your intention is to stay on top of things, you must continue to learn and explore both Cubase and new programs.

> **NOTE**
>
> You should periodically check Steinberg's web site to keep up to date with the latest software versions.

Don't let this scare you off. Embrace the changes and realize that even though they may seem strange at first, they are always the result of good intentions by the program's developers. Cubase is constantly aiming to make the music-creation process easier and better for the end user (you!). If there are changes that you would like to see in the program in the future, you should contact Steinberg. Who knows? You could actually affect the development of the music software that will create the music of tomorrow.

Appendix A

Working with Multiple MIDI Tracks in an Editor

One of the great things about working in Cubase's MIDI editors is that you can work with multiple MIDI tracks at once. This can be very helpful for making sure your parts are working together the way they should. Any two or more parts selected at the same time in the project window can be opened and edited simultaneously in the Key editor, List editor, Drum editor, or Score editor. Cubase's tools function the same working with multiple tracks as they do when working with one track.

To get the hang of working with multiple tracks at once, close any projects currently open in Cubase and open Song5. This example focuses on the Electric Piano and Funk Guitar parts in the Key editor. The parts in this example have been separated by color using the Color Scheme selector. The Electric Piano part is pink, and the Funk Guitar is a powder blue. Notice that there is a velocity controller lane displayed at the bottom of the Key editor.

Using the Part Display

When you work with multiple MIDI tracks, you can only view one part's controller lanes at a time. In this example, if you want to see the controller lanes for the Electric Piano part, you need to select that part.

There are two ways to select a part. One is to use the OST to select a note in the part you want to work with. When the note is selected, the part also becomes selected, and the controller lanes for that part appear below the Note display. Another way to select a part is to use the part display located on the toolbar. For the sake of example, open the part display's drop-down menu; you'll see a part for funk guitar and another part for electric piano. Select the part you want to view from the list; Cubase displays the controllers for that part below the Note display.

> **NOTE**
>
> When working with multiple parts, you can *create* notes for only one part at a time. First select the part in the part display, and then create a note for that part using the Pencil tool, Line tool, MIDI keyboard, or step input as normal. In this example, if you wanted to create some new electric piano notes, you would first select the Electric Piano part.

Edit the Active Part Only

While editing both parts, you may find it tricky to work with several parts at once. This is especially tricky when the parts are playing the same notes at the same time. In these cases, the Edit Active Part Only button comes in really handy. The following is an example to show you how this works:

1. Select the Solo Editor button. That way, if you want to play the track, you'll be able to concentrate on the Electric Piano and the Funk Guitar parts.

> **NOTE**
>
> When working with multiple parts, the Solo Editor button plays all the parts you are working with. That means if you want to see multiple parts but only hear one part, you should mute the part you don't want to hear. Muting a whole part is easier to do in the project window.

2. With the Edit Active Part Only button off, use the OST to select both the F3 and the D#3 notes of the electric piano and the funk guitar at measure 11, beat 2.2 simultaneously.

3. Using the OST, move the two notes to the right one space on the grid so that they are both at measure 11, beat 2.3 without changing their respective pitches. You've just edited multiple notes on two separate parts. This should appear as in the example in Figure A.1.

4. Select the Edit Active Part Only button from the toolbar.

5. Click anywhere in the Note display so that the two notes you just moved are no longer selected.

6. Use the OST to select both notes.

7. What's the matter? Can't you select both notes? Of course you can't! The Edit Active Part Only button enables you to edit only one part at a time, and the part it lets you select is the part that is active in the toolbar's part display.

You can try to delete, move, or change the lengths of the Funk Guitar part, but nothing will happen as long as the Edit Active Part Only button is activated and the electric piano is chosen in the part display. If you were to choose the funk guitar in the part display with the Edit Active Part Only button activated, you would no longer be able to edit the Electric Piano part. This is a safety feature to protect you from changing parts you don't want to change.

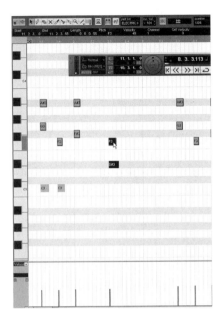

Figure A.1
The electric piano and funk guitar notes have been moved.

NOTE

Unlike the Solo Editor button, which works with multiple parts, the Independent Track Loop button only loops the part displayed in the part display. This seems like a bug that hopefully Cubase will work out, because it could be a nice feature to use with multiple parts. Also, it appears that the Chord Viewer cannot calculate chords for multiple parts at once and only refers to the part that is selected in the part display. For those who want to make sure their multiple parts aren't creating a proverbial harmonic train wreck, this would be a nice feature to have in the future, but for now it's not possible.

Editing multiple tracks in the List editor and Drum editor is handled in a similar way as it is in the Key editor. Editing multiple tracks in the Score editor is different because each track is represented on its own stave, making the process a little less complicated and the need to use the part display obsolete.

Appendix B

More Shortcuts

N ow that you know how to edit MIDI in every way possible in Cubase 4, there are a few steps you can take to save yourself some time.

Keyboard Shortcuts

Using your computer keyboard (as opposed to the mouse) can be a great way to speed up the process of working in Cubase. Indeed, Cubase has devoted a whole chapter to using key commands in the user's manual; you can find an impressive list of default commands on pages 438–440. If you can memorize them all, you will indeed be a true Cubase Grand Master.

It's also possible to change the default keys to a key on the keyboard that suits your needs. When you have all your key commands in order, you can save your settings under one preset name so that you can change your settings later and recall your original settings at any time. Cubase also comes with key-command presets from other versions of Cubase as well as the default settings for Logic.

Macros

Using macros works similarly to using key commands but speeds up multiple tasks even more by enabling you to handle more than one task with one simple mouse click. Here's a brief guide to creating a macro command:

1. Open Song16 on the CD-ROM accompanying this book.

2. Open the File menu and choose Key Commands.

3. In the Key Command dialog box, click Show Macros.

4. Select New Macro to display the New Command field.

5. In the New Command field, type `Once Again, But Faster`.

6. In the Command window above the macros display, locate and open the Edit folder.

7. In the Edit folder, locate and select the Duplicate command.

8. Click Add Command. The command is added underneath the macro you created.

9. Close the Edit folder and locate and open the Process Logical Preset folder in the Command window.

10. In the Process Logical Preset folder, select Double Tempo.

11. Click Add Command. The Double Tempo command is added under the Duplicate command.

12. Click OK. Congrats! You've created a macro.

13. In Song16, select the entire song (three drum tracks).

14. Open the Edit menu, choose Macros, and select your new macro, Once Again, But Faster. The three tracks are duplicated, and the duplicate is made at double tempo.

This handy-dandy macro has just saved you a couple of steps, and you can use it as often as you want. Every possible command is located within the list of commands, so it's possible to create some pretty specific macros if needed.

The Pop-Up Menu

As mentioned in previous chapters, there are a lot of shortcut possibilities when using the pop-up menu that appears when you right-click the display window of any editor (see Figure B.1).

Figure B.1

The pop-up menu.

The contents of this pop-up menu change, depending on what editor you're working with and what is currently selected, just as the items listed in the menu bar change to show what you can or cannot use at the current time (that is, entries are grayed out when they are not available for use). For the most part, anything you can do from the Edit menu (located in the menu bar), you can do using the Edit, Range, Select, Zoom, and Move To submenus in the pop-up menu. Likewise, you can execute many of the commands in the Project menu (including the command that opens the Project browser) from the Project and Add Track submenus. Also available in the pop-up menu are the MIDI functions available from the MIDI menu, including Advanced Quantize options and quick access to the Score editor. Finally, the pop-up menu provides an alternative way of showing the Info Line (instead of using the Show Info Line button). Other menu options that aren't MIDI related also appear.

The Transport

You can access a lot of quick playback options, most of which are pretty self explanatory, from the Transport menu on the menu bar or from the pop-up menu. Alternatively, you can use the small row of controls, called the *transport*, located over the track display (see Figure B.2).

Figure B.2

The track controls over the track display.

Using these track controls not only gives you quick access to the track control settings, it also offers you a quick way to open the In-Place editor for the selected tracks, the ability to un-mute or un-solo all muted or soloed tracks, and the ability to enable read and write automation on all tracks at once. There is also a handy color tool that displays a color line next to the track; you can easily change track colors by clicking the line and changing the color using the pop-up color palette. The Divide Track List button lets you separate different types of tracks so that you can change your zoom according to the type of track you are focused on.

Cubase supports the use of many other shortcuts; in addition, you can create new ones yourself by changing your Preferences setup. Although this book covered a great number of features, in the Cubase manual, Chapter 36, "Customizing," provides a few more ways to change and save your workspace, change the appearance of Cubase, and save your preferences so that Cubase works the way you need it to. To access the preferences, open the File menu and select Preferences.

Index

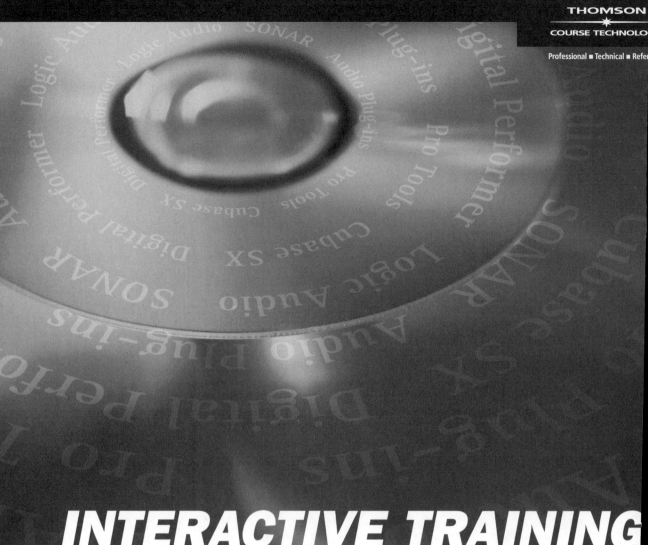

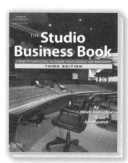

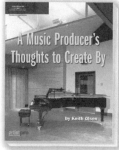

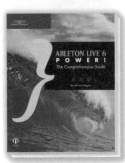

License Agreement/Notice of Limited Warranty

By opening the sealed disc container in this book, you agree to the following terms and conditions. If, upon reading the following license agreement and notice of limited warranty, you cannot agree to the terms and conditions set forth, return the unused book with unopened disc to the place where you purchased it for a refund.

License:

The enclosed software is copyrighted by the copyright holder(s) indicated on the software disc. You are licensed to copy the software onto a single computer for use by a single user and to a backup disc. You may not reproduce, make copies, or distribute copies or rent or lease the software in whole or in part, except with written permission of the copyright holder(s). You may transfer the enclosed disc only together with this license, and only if you destroy all other copies of the software and the transferee agrees to the terms of the license. You may not decompile, reverse assemble, or reverse engineer the software.

Notice of Limited Warranty:

The enclosed disc is warranted by Thomson Course Technology PTR to be free of physical defects in materials and workmanship for a period of sixty (60) days from end user's purchase of the book/disc combination. During the sixty-day term of the limited warranty, Thomson Course Technology PTR will provide a replacement disc upon the return of a defective disc.

Limited Liability:

THE SOLE REMEDY FOR BREACH OF THIS LIMITED WARRANTY SHALL CONSIST ENTIRELY OF REPLACEMENT C THE DEFECTIVE DISC. IN NO EVENT SHALL THOMSON COURSE TECHNOLOGY PTR OR THE AUTHOR BE LIABLE FOR ANY OTHER DAMAGES, INCLUDING LOSS OR CORRUPTION OF DATA, CHANGES IN THE FUNCTIONAL CHARACTERISTICS OF THE HARDWARE OR OPERATING SYSTEM, DELETERIOUS INTERACTION WITH OTHER SOFTWARE, OR ANY OTHER SPECIAL, INCIDENTAL, OR CONSEQUENTIAL DAMAGES THAT MAY ARISE, EVEN I THOMSON COURSE TECHNOLOGY PTR AND/OR THE AUTHOR HAS PREVIOUSLY BEEN NOTIFIED THAT THE POSSIBILITY OF SUCH DAMAGES EXISTS.

Disclaimer of Warranties:

THOMSON COURSE TECHNOLOGY PTR AND THE AUTHOR SPECIFICALLY DISCLAIM ANY AND ALL OTHER WARRANTIES, EITHER EXPRESS OR IMPLIED, INCLUDING WARRANTIES OF MERCHANTABILITY, SUITABILITY TO A PARTICULAR TASK OR PURPOSE, OR FREEDOM FROM ERRORS. SOME STATES DO NOT ALLOW FOR EXCLUSION OF IMPLIED WARRANTIES OR LIMITATION OF INCIDENTAL OR CONSEQUENTIAL DAMAGES, SO THESE LIMITATIONS MIGHT NOT APPLY TO YOU.

Other:

This Agreement is governed by the laws of the State of Massachusetts without regard to choice of law principles. The United Convention of Contracts for the International Sale of Goods is specifically disclaimed. This Agreement constitutes the entire agreement between you and Thomson Course Technology PTR regarding use of the software.